JOHN POWELL WARD

Thomas Hardy's Poetry

Open University Press
Buckingham · Philadelphia

Open University Press
Celtic Court
22 Ballmoor
Buckingham
MK18 1XW

and
1900 Frost Road, Suite 101
Bristol, PA 19007, USA

First Published 1993

A catalogue record of this book is available from the British Library

Library of Congress Cataloging-in-Publication Data

Ward, John Powell, 1937–
    Thomas Hardy's poetry / John Powell Ward.
        p.   cm. – (Open guides to literature)
    Includes bibliographical references and index.
    ISBN 0–335–09991–2   ISBN 0–335–09990–4 (pbk.)
    1. Hardy, Thomas, 1840–1928–Poetic works.   I. Title.
II. Series.
PR4757.P58W37   1992
821′.8 – dc20   92-14301
                                                                CIP

Typeset by Best-set Typesetter Limited, Hong Kong
Printed in Great Britain by J.W. Arrowsmith Limited, Bristol

PONTEFRACT

8.99

Open Guides to Literature

Series Editor: Graham Martin (Professor of Literature, The Open University)

Titles in the Series

Contents

Series Editor's Preface

The intention of this series is to provide short introductory books about major writers, texts, and literary concepts for students of courses in Higher Education which substantially or wholly involve the study of Literature.

The series adopts a pedagogic approach and style similar to that of Open University Material for Literature courses. *Open Guides* aim to inculcate the reading 'skills' which many introductory books in the field tend, mistakenly, to assume that the reader already possesses. They are, in this sense, 'teacherly' texts, planned and written in a manner which will develop in the reader the confidence to undertake further independent study of the topic. They are 'open' in two senses. First, they offer a three-way tutorial exchange between the writer of the *Guide*, the text or texts in question, and the reader. They invite readers to join in an exploratory discussion of texts, concentrating on their key aspects and on the main problems which readers, coming to the texts for the first time, are likely to encounter. The flow of a *Guide* 'discourse' is established by putting questions for the reader to follow up in a tentative and searching spirit, guided by the writer's comments, but not dominated by an over-arching and single-mindedly pursued argument or evaluation, which itself requires to be 'read'.

Guides are also 'open' in a second sense. They assume that literary texts are 'plural', that there is no end to interpretation, and that it is for the reader to undertake the pleasurable task of discovering meaning and value in such texts. *Guides* seek to provide, in compact form, such relevant biographical, historical and cultural information as bears upon the reading of the text, and they point the reader to a selection of the best available critical discussions of it. They are not in themselves concerned to propose, or to counter, particular readings of the texts, but rather to put *Guide* readers in a position to do that for themselves. Experienced travellers learn to dispense with guides, and so it should be for readers of this series.

Graham Martin

Author's Note

This book has been written to be used with the following text:

> *Thomas Hardy: Selected Poems*, edited with an Introduction by David Wright, The Penguin Poetry Library (Harmondsworth: Penguin, 1978).

This selection contains well over three hundred of the poems. The poems are not arranged chronologically. All but one of the poems discussed or referred to in the present book can be found in this Penguin edition. (The single exception, 'The Garden Seat', is printed in full where discussion of it occurs in the text.)

When poems are discussed or mentioned in this book, they are normally not quoted, except for brief illustrative lines or passages in a few cases. You therefore need either this edition or one of the complete editions listed below with you when you are using this book. The page number of the Penguin edition where each poem can be found is given on the first citing of that poem in any one chapter.

There are two complete editions of Thomas Hardy's poems:

> *Thomas Hardy: The Complete Poems*, edited by James Gibson (London: Macmillan, 1976 and 1981).
> This was published in hardback as the New Wessex Edition in 1976, and in paperback, by Papermac, in 1981. It includes all the poetry apart from *The Dynasts*.

> *Thomas Hardy: The Complete Poetical Works*, edited in 3 volumes by Samuel Hynes (Oxford: The Clarendon Press, 1985).

> These volumes are only available in hardback.

Acknowledgements

Many thanks to Furze Swann, of the Thomas Hardy Society, for his kind welcome; and to Graham Martin, of the Open University, for his support and encouragement. I am greatly indebted to William Morgan, of Illinois State University, for making available to me prior to publication his research on the dating of Hardy's poems.

1. First Selection

In this opening chapter, without any preliminary on background, literary theory or anything else, let's go direct to some Hardy poems.

Even to do that however, especially if Hardy's poetry is new to you, needs a warning. Thomas Hardy wrote over a thousand poems. They are mainly short; often a page or less in length, although an important minority are longer. But the thousand poems themselves pose a problem of selection right at the start. For Hardy, unlike most poets, wrote with a certain homogeneity or 'sameness' right across his work, so that it is often difficult to know how to focus it, or how to go to clear identifiable groups; or even clear successes and failures.

Critics differ on this matter, and a number feel that the degree of this supposed sameness, or lack of progressive development, has been exaggerated. Yet anyone familiar with the body of Hardy's poetry will I think know what we are referring to here; and it simply means that, for someone stepping out on Hardy's poetry, you do need to be ready to read quite a lot of poems. That is the emphasis we need to make here. Have no fear; most are very short, they read fairly easily, and are often narrative in form. That at least is a provisional opening statement; for of course, the question of just how simple 'simple' is, comes up with many writers. But it does mean that quite often in this book, including in this opening chapter, I will suggest two or three poems to read as examples of our immediate topic, instead of just one. At times, later on, I will list a whole pile of poems to exemplify various matters, even if we don't discuss them all. I don't think you will find this oppressive. The more you read of them, the more you will get into it, and indeed it is a phenomenon very familiar to readers of Hardy's poetry, that you gradually get to a point where you can more or less 'flow' from one poem into another as you read. So get used to the idea and the habit, from the word go, of reading more in number than you might with other poets.

One more initial point before we start. The idea in this book will be that readers should discover as much as possible for themselves. (Please make sure you have read the note on the texts, which appears at the end of the Series Preface.) This gives a sense of confidence, of achievement, of pleasure, and perhaps most of all, the priceless value of taking possession of some cultural item on one's own; such treasures can last a lifetime. Yet having said all that, we have to start somewhere, and so I, as author, at this point must make one or two assumptions about the poetry and what it is about. I don't think anyone reading Hardy's poetry would ever deny that much of it is about love and death; it has most extraordinary curiosities as to its language, grammar and structure; and it is powerfully visual. So Chapters 3 to 6 in this book are each about one of those four aspects: *seeing*; *love*; *death*; and *language*.

It remains only to add that Hardy also wrote a very long poem, *The Dynasts*, some seven hundred pages long in the standard edition; he also published (depending what you count) something like fifteen full-length novels. Except in passing, we won't touch the novels or *The Dynasts* in this book. Later on our discussion will widen. Matters arise from the poetry about the modern world generally: industry, godlessness and science; the passing of time; nature; human love; sorrow, futility and sadness. Just what leads on to what, we shall discuss when we have looked at the topics of seeing, love, death and language. For the moment though, let's have a first look at some poems about these opening four matters.

Here then are some poems that seem to highlight the first of these matters particularly: 'seeing'; the visually encountered. They are 'Snow in the Suburbs', 'Overlooking the River Stour' and 'A Light Snow-Fall after Frost'. They are found on pages 225, 346 and 168 of the Penguin edition. First, consider the difference between the first two of these poems. 'Snow in the Suburbs' would appear to be straightforward natural description of the precise way the snow falls on to the bushes and hangs there. By line three the poet has already brought our eyes in close by seeing the snow clinging to a forked twig as with a 'web-foot', and I am sure that – even in unsnowy Britain – most of us have seen how falling snowflakes seem to have 'lost their way' as they swirl about in an icy wind, deflecting them from their downward course. Then in stanza two is the humorous business of the lump of snow falling on and all but burying the chirpy little sparrow (made to seem comically human, perhaps, by being called 'him' rather than 'it').

On the face of it, 'Overlooking the River Stour' seems simply another piece of careful, natural description. But the last stanza then changes everything. Having being just as visually close and detailed about the swallows and buttercups as he was about the snow, the poet now suddenly, and it seems deeply, even in panic, regrets seeing these things. He thinks instead of those that were going on 'behind my back' while he was looking out over the river, and which he never tells us about. Indeed he calls the invisible events or sights behind him 'more', the river scene 'less'.

What is happening here? Well, we might wonder. It is tempting just to enjoy the poem; but some intriguing features do surely arise. As with the snow poem, the poet really does seem to dwell on the outward world's features, and very successfully. The swallows as 'little crossbows animate', the water-bird landing on the river (like a sea-plane) 'Planing up shavings' of spray; those are very accurate, felicitous comparisons. So whatever happened behind him, must have been of some importance to end up more significant still. But, by the time he comes to write the poem itself, he knows that; he knows what resulted. So why emphasize so much of what, in the end, turned out to be less important? Perhaps precisely to underline the poignant tragedy of the very failure to direct his attention where it was most needed. And in any event, what *did* happen 'behind his back'? Here is where biographical approaches to literary criticism start raising their heads (we know when Hardy wrote this, and how he was getting on); but let's leave them aside for the present. Staying simply with the poem, what happened? Was there some dreadful event the poet missed and could have prevented, if only he had attended where he should have, instead of glutting himself on nature's pleasures? Or was it that he was merely being selfish, neglecting some lonely person behind his back? Or could 'behind his back' be a much more general metaphor, to stand in for all of life's wider busy events, which his escapism led him to miss?

What one might also notice, surely, is the way that the first and last couplet in each stanza is repeated. This lends a chanting, dreamy, even wistful quality to the poem's feeling, as though the poet is sardonically or sadly laughing at himself for his excessive powers of observation. He could have been adding more observations in the space used up by those lines. Instead, by repeating them, he knowingly curtails his seeing power, and lets in a more human apprehension. And this is what I wanted to underline in

comparing these first two poems. The power and the habit of
'seeing' raise feelings in the poet's mind as to what such powers
are for, or what brought them on. You can't just sit and look at
things as a camera does *even if* you seem to have that power. That
very power is itself what leads you on to see other implications,
other limits and dangers. For a comparable poem that looks in
detail at a scene and then seems to realize it has missed something
else – something more human – you might like to consider 'On
the Esplanade' (p. 323). We will look further at 'On the Esplanade'
in a later chapter.

The third poem, 'A Light Snow-Fall after Frost', also refers to
what happens when you watch a natural event. Here the poet
seems to want to guard himself against jumping to conclusions
from the very start. He is already saying, in stanza one, that 'One
cannot certify' how much the white hair of a man walking along
a snowy road comes from his age or from the thin 'settling' snow
itself. And this is already a new dimension, for 'life's rough
pilgrimage'; that which brings on whitening hair, is a matter of
pain and experience. Is this why, do you think, the poem calmly
declares with even greater certainty that we cannot tell when
things change? When a road in a snowfall goes from brown to
white, or when a friend's hair is normal or grey, when he or she
in fact have ceased to look young? This is an intriguing poem –
one often used in Hardy explication by critics – for its various
elements cut across each other. It seems that the one thing clearly
seen, the man in stanza three, has colour; red hair and a green
jacket (in passing, invariably reminding the present writer of Van
Gogh). Colour is rare in Hardy's poems. Offhand, I can think of
only three or four others that refer to it. But this red and green
perhaps implies that the life and richness of colour give us human
purchase on what we see, while mere shades of white cannot.
And contrasting these two men, unlike in the other two poems we
considered, there is a 'watcher', the person who can't tell the
natural changes. Is that 'watcher' again a clue; that only to watch,
without entering humanly in, is what keeps us back from human
understanding, from how people's looks are affected by their
feelings? Is that reading too much into it? Or is it, rather, merely
what it seems, a poem about cognition and epistemology themselves; about the psychology of perception, the way we can't say
if the famous drawing is a rabbit or a duck, a vase or two
confronting faces?

I hope all this will have indicated that Hardy, it seems, is a
poet who watches, sees and stares, and is led by that very habit
into wondering what he has seen, what it has felt like, and what it

has told him. It's enough, here, to say that he sometimes suggested it was more like being blind. Why? We will consider the poetry's visual aspect in a later chapter.

Then there is the matter of love. You may have read David Wright's introduction to the Penguin edition. He says there (pp. 22 and following) that Hardy's overwhelming topic is love and marriage; over three hundred poems. I am not sure it overwhelms the other topics (death, science) as much as that; but Hardy was undeniably obsessed with women and with love. Again, however, let us omit the biographical story for the present and take some poems. May I suggest you now read 'Faintheart in a Railway Train' (p. 317) and 'A Hurried Meeting' (p. 176).

As we shall see in the next chapter, Hardy's attitude to love is very much coloured by the circumstances of his meeting his eventual wife Emma Gifford, the long marriage itself, and her death and his reaction to it. Admittedly his love poems seem to cover a wide range of tone and circumstance. For example, many poems respond to women he saw by chance, probably once only, in the countryside or across a street. Yet the majority do turn out to have something in common perhaps, and these two just named may, in their quite different ways, begin to throw light on a common attitude or disposition.

Take the first, 'Faintheart in a Railway Train'. Does it seem to you just a little peculiar? We have just seen – from the 'seeing' poems – that Hardy's attention to and attraction for the details of the natural landscape were very great; yet here he rushes through church, sea, town and forest in four lines. Intentionally so, of course, yet more curious still is that, if we are to believe the second word of each line in the first stanza, this occurred on a train journey which spread over at least five hours. The only thing that tempts him 'out' is a single glance at an admittedly pretty girl. But, even if we allow the extravagance that sexual attraction and a sense of exhilaration can give, is it remotely to be conceived that he would have broken a presumably fairly important journey – since he had to go so far – to meet someone who might have proved unattractive, already bespoke, wholly uninterested, or generally quite unsuitable? Are we really to credit that he is not only regretful but self-abasing at his lack of daring? Is the wistful longing in the last two lines, then, not merely self-indulgence?

Perhaps we shouldn't take the poem too seriously, although as a comparable but rather more significant episode you might like to look at 'A Thunderstorm in Town' (p. 358). Hardy said once that he was always astonished at those beautiful women you might see at any moment, on the street or in a shop, just as beautiful as any society belle, yet faceless, belonging nowhere. Perhaps this poem merely records a brief case of that, or a whimsy about it. But in any event, a rather different level of engagement is found in 'A Hurried Meeting'. What strikes us about this? What is different, as well as obviously different, from the first poem? The first stanza has more detailed description of the setting than is provided in the whole of the other poem. Does that put the spotlight on these unfortunate lovers in some way? Is it that they can't escape their setting any longer, that all is now in the open glare of the moonlight?

What surely strikes us about all three poems is that in some way or another love seems to fall short. In Chapter 4 we will consider whether that is general in Hardy's love-poems. In this opening chapter I only want to suggest that many of the love poems seem to be situational. We get, not so much a general declaration of love, or sadness at its ending, but an incident or event in which it occurred or failed to occur. This, it turns out, is what so often accompanies lack or failure in love. The poet is not declaring himself to his love, or rapturously expounding her beauty to the stars. Indeed, apart from the magisterial aristocracy of the woman in this poem – and her backing mansion – we might even see these two poems as a before-and-after picture of the poet's same prototype love. The first poem is obsessional – he sees no scenery and can think only of his failure to approach the girl. The second poem is disillusioned and wide-awake; he sees *all* the scenery, the social circumstances, the wretched outcome, the desperate undignified planning. Now we can't take this further at present, but if you look at some of Hardy's other love-poems now, for instance 'The Wind's Prophecy' (p. 331), 'Beyond the Last Lamp' (p. 167), 'A Thunderstorm in Town' already mentioned, you might care to ask how this situational quality, apparently so often present, strikes you. It is so often associated with failure in love. How different it is from for example Shakespeare's sonnets, when we hardly know of any situation at all. Hardy does, on other occasions, seem to sing the lyric song (for example 'If It's Ever Spring Again', p. 222) or see love more optimistically ('A Church Romance', p. 60), but it is rare, and even then there is often a compromising factor; as in for example 'After the Visit' (p. 403), where the title alone seems to pull the poem back from pure love relationship. On other occasions, though, it is only death that calms the love into quietude ('Two Lips', p. 401, 'She Hears the Storm', p. 70).

And death is another ubiquitous theme in Hardy's poetry. One might say it reeks of it. Why is there this obsession? Yet, here again, we find different approaches to the matter, at least on the face of it. If you have just read 'She Hears the Storm' you might pair it briefly with 'On the Doorstep' (p. 400). In both cases one aim of the poem is to avoid mentioning death as such. By contrast poems like 'Channel Firing' (p. 278) positively revel in their absorption in the below-ground condition of the deceased. Does this suggest that death, like love, is an obsession for Hardy, and that he will always strive to express it, no matter what different forms it takes?

In 'She Hears the Storm' what stands out is the catalogue of natural and other phenomena, listed mainly in the third and fourth stanza, which the surviving widow will no longer have to concern herself with. This seems rather dwelt-on, if not exactly obsessional, but it contrasts oddly with the fact that the 'nature' which brings on all these anxieties of storm and tempest, is the same nature that provides the 'roof', the tomb or grave, which then protects against it. I mention this here as preliminary to later discussion of a very famous poem of Hardy's, 'Friends Beyond' (p. 182). There, the catalogue of things that fade away after death is a matter more of man-made than natural cares and pressures. We shall have to ask later how far this incessant dwelling on death is a kind of comment on life, on what we do have to cope with in this world.

Although about death, the word is not mentioned in the poem; one could even, I suppose, find another interpretation of it. But in 'On the Doorstep' not naming death seems even more pointed. We are left to realize what is meant ourselves. How does that strike you? We can hardly say the poet shrinks from mentioning death in at least its symbolic details, for skeletons, graveyards and ghosts abound in much of the death poetry he writes. There is, for example, 'A Merrymaking in Question' (p. 97) and 'Reminiscences of a Dancing Man' (p. 97), where explicit reference to such details might seem positively chilling to some readers. As we shall see, Hardy is at times absorbed with our mortal remains and what happens to them. How effective then is this other, much more indirect treatment in 'On the Doorstep', do you think, where only at the end does it dawn on us that death is the topic?

Of course, in this poem the poet is presented (in stanza one) as hearing only the 'song' of whoever he lived with. There is no fuller relationship. So in stanza two the sudden sense that the song is gone is what strikes him. But he presents even that to the reader only by 'no song-notes'; a negative. But, while there is no necessary inconsistency, this does sharply contrast with what we find in certain other poems. In some poems the dead speak, and they may even be named. Is this a different aspect of death Hardy is giving us? Hardy's ghosts are a renowned feature of his poetic work. Did he believe in them? Again I leave that for you to think about, and form your own views, at least provisionally, as you read more poems (e.g. try 'Who's in the Next Room?', p. 303 and 'The Ghost of the Past', p. 61) before we elaborate on this matter of death in the poetry in Chapter 5.

Most of what we have said so far has been on the poems as content; as though *what* they said could be separated from how, or written in prose without loss. But of course that is commonly not possible, nor perhaps desirable, with poetry. So let's turn finally, in this opening chapter, to the style and tone of Hardy's poetic writing, its quirks of vocabulary and grammar, and its strange apparent awkwardnesses. There have been several examples in the poems we have already looked at.

The critical response to this aspect of Hardy's 'awkwardness' since the height of his poetic work appeared in the 1920s has, broadly speaking, gone in two phases. For the first fifteen or so years the feeling was that as a poet he was clumsy and unskilled, and that his lack of formal education meant that he failed to express his undeniable poetic feeling for human circumstance in a competent enough style. The feeling today, by contrast, is that his apparent clumsiness comes from the most subtle poetic craft, and that his own remarks on the subject – for example that all art must contain much deliberate imperfection to avoid falsity, or that all art must seem a little offhand – must now be taken seriously.

If you hadn't read Hardy's work before, what did you think of the effect of the selection we have now considered, in terms of its style? Does it make sense for example that Hardy himself felt that 'the whole secret of a living style ... lies in not having too much style – being, in fact, a little careless, or rather seeming to be'?[1] Was the view of F. R. Leavis a dissent from it: 'the verse has little intrinsic value: Hardy's great poetry is a triumph of character'?[2] Can any great poetry have 'little intrinsic virtue'? And what of a comment like that of the novelist Somerset Maugham, who appeared to suggest that Hardy's poems had been written with the stub of a blunt pencil?[3] Some clear examples of what was meant occur in the poems we have already looked at.

'Faintheart in a Railway Train' yields up some clear, brief examples.

> At nine in the morning there passed a church,
> At ten there passed me by the sea,
> At twelve a town of smoke and smirch,
> At two a forest of oak and birch,
>   And then, on a platform, she:
>
> A radiant stranger, who saw not me.
> I said, 'Get out to her do I dare?'
> But I kept my seat in my search for a plea,
> And the wheels moved on. O could it but be
>   That I had alighted there!

At the simplest, Hardy often apparently puts in a word just to get a rhyme, or turns a sentence round ('inverted grammatical word-order') equally just to get a rhyme. Here, there is 'smirch' (to rhyme with 'church') and 'Get out to her do I dare?' (for 'do I dare to get out to her?') to rhyme with 'there'. There is also the curious open-ended, at first sight rather feeble expression 'my search for a plea', in 'But I kept my seat in my search for a plea'. This presumably means that the poet stayed in his seat while he tried to think of a pretext for speaking to her. And there has already been the equally odd, though this time grammatically correct 'she', at the end of a line, where we might have expected 'a girl' or something similar. In contrast to these examples though is the internal rhyme of 'smoke and smirch' with 'oak and birch', catching the jogging effect of the train; and the surely vivid choice of 'wheels', where the routine word 'train' would have been so easy, rhythmically correct, and plain dull. In that light 'she' suddenly feels sharp and quick, and surprises us as the girl perhaps struck Hardy. The point of the poem's writing then, perhaps, is not that it is awkward, amateur, and so on, but that no one would ever say it; and this is apt here because when we are being jogged along in a bumpy train our natural flow of talk does become jarred.

If this is 'awkward', we can at least claim that Hardy doesn't mind, rather than that he could do no better. The effect of the poem is quite clear. The small scene on the country station is vivid and immediate. Now if we glance again at 'Overlooking the River Stour' and 'A Hurried Meeting', we see that the palpable vocabulary, the solid words that make the scene vivid, are where the surprises lie. In the first poem 'gleam' and 'beam' are both strangely abrupt, yet for that very reason the more noticeable. And, looking at the window-pane in the rain with its 'drop-drenched glaze';

well, what do you think? Is it awkward, or perhaps brilliantly economic? Other words or phrases you might consider are 'cross-bows animate', 'curves of an eight' and 'thereabout' all incidentally ending with 't', which Hardy does seem fond of.

In 'A Hurried Meeting' 'outscreen', 'heart-outeating' and particularly 'obscure' (adjective as noun, a common Hardy trick) are worth noting. There is also the terse phrase with no main verb 'Inferior clearly he', and the whole line that ends the first stanza, 'And the trees seem to withhold their softest breathing'. Is that a little too thought-out? Does it congest, or compel? Your choice.

In a later chapter we will look at many more examples of how this strange language manifests itself, and ask what it is supposed to do and what it tells us about Hardy's very idea of language. To anyone who feels like writing him off as clumsy one might reply again, 'your choice'. But a sobering thought is that by the time most of these poems were written (and at least some of those mentioned here) Hardy had written and successfully published about fifteen novels. That's a lot of practice in supple-ness of phrase; we should at least give him a hearing.

So there are some opening thoughts about Hardy's poetry. There's a lot more to it, of course; it isn't all love and death, neutrally seen and weirdly expressed. Hardy felt deeply the in-dustrial encroachments of his century, the changing social and religious philosophy of his time, and the impact of technological war. But before going into these things more closely a sketch of his life will be helpful. It can point us in certain useful directions – which we will take note of on the way – and also, among other things, the general question of how far such biographical material may be used as an aid to understanding a poet's work.

2. Main Events
in the Life

Thomas Hardy was born just outside Dorchester in 1840. That made 1990 the 150th anniversary of his birth, when there were celebrations in various parts of the world, notably in Dorchester itself. The Festival Service took place in St Peter's Church, Dorchester in July 1990. I was fortunate enough to be there; and the address was given by the present Bishop of Salisbury. This was appropriate enough, for despite a later loss of faith doctrinally, Hardy always loved the Church of England, its architecture and liturgy; he was an orthodox Anglican by upbringing; and Dorchester is in the Salisbury diocese. But the bishop's suitability turned out to be even more marked. He said: 'It so happens that Thomas Hardy's life and my own neatly join to cover the 150 years which are the occasion for this celebration, for I was born in the early hours of the very same day on which, at 9.00 in the evening, he passed away'.[1] The day in question was 11 January 1928.

A nice moment; but this was more than merely a whimsically interesting coincidence. Hardy was himself fascinated by the way that long stretches of time can seem bridged by noting whose life overlapped whose. He once remarked that while the poet William Wordsworth (1770–1850) could conceivably have seen young Thomas in his pram, or even a little later, so too could the poet Thomas Gray (1716–1771) (a Hardy favourite) have spotted William.[2] Total time (let's include the bishop too): over two hundred and ten years.

Such anecdotes bring out a unique feature of Hardy's literary career. His *first* book of poems was published when he was fifty-eight, late in the day on anyone's reckoning; yet he lived a further thirty years, producing eight more books of poetry and, as we

have said, over a thousand poems. This raises another remarkable
fact, for Hardy had already put *two* careers in what may properly
be called the arts behind him. Before his fifteen or more novels he
had already spent some years as an architect. There are a number
of poems concerned with architecture, particularly 'The Abbey-
Mason' (p. 130), referred to later in this chapter. Important too at
home in Hardy's childhood had been music. His father sang and
played the violin, Hardy did the latter himself, and scores of his
poems, years hence, contain echoes of old ballads, popular songs,
and hymns. I should say here that, in the course of this largely
biographical chapter, I will mention a number of poems in passing,
in order to get a general orientation toward the work. Please note
that you are not expected to read these poems now and that later
chapters will not assume you have done so. Of course if you do,
well and good, and any that you do read will help build your
understanding of Hardy, as well as (I hope) give you pleasure. But
the main reason for mentioning them was given in Chapter 1;
namely, that Hardy wrote so many poems that we need to get a
good selection into the story at various points.

The standard biographies of Thomas Hardy are by Robert
Gittings and Michael Millgate.[3] You can see that whatever else
they are they are long. The present chapter will do no more than
pick on the main events and periods from Hardy's life which seem
to inform the poetry. Speaking for myself, I do sometimes wonder
whether certain poems are – no, not spoiled, but somehow
diminished by our knowing too exactly when and where they were
written, and who for or about. Yet more generally, life and work
must necessarily be connected, and there may be some poems
in which an apparent biographical reference is too clear to be
coincidence. The real danger is of forgetting that the poet may
have transposed fact into imagination and fiction. We should not
assume *a priori* that a poem relates an event that occurred, and
just as it occurred. If that is clear, we need not fear that a good
poem will be submerged by biographical facts. The length of
Hardy's life, and his poetic late start, is one such fact. Let's now
list the others.

1 *Childhood and adolescence.* Hardy was born in the country
near Dorchester in 1840 and raised there. His family were
Dorset people, and he was much interested in the presence of
Hardys across the county. His father was a builder; he was
himself brought up in the church and was thoroughly familiar
with the Bible and the Anglican liturgy.

2 *Young architect.* He was an architect's apprentice and then

paid assistant in Dorchester from 1856 to 1862, and then went to London. He was a keen and good architect, interested particularly in churches and other ancient buildings.

3 *Women*. Hardy was perennially attracted to women, preferably young, but sometimes older than himself. It has been said of him that he was the kind of man to fall at once in love with women he met quite by chance, and this continued well into his later life.

4 *Literary career*. Despite the architecture, he was thinking of a literary career quite early. He bought much poetry, and dictionaries and grammars, and in the 1860s apparently wrote more poetry than he was to do for some decades. So when, in his mid-fifties, he turned to poetry centrally there was already a body of work in existence, though very little published. Nevertheless, he elected to try the novel, largely because it offered more realistic hope of making a living. His first published novel, *Desperate Remedies*, was accepted for publication in 1870.

5 *Marriage*. 1870 was crucial in another respect. On a trip to St Juliot's in Cornwall concerned with restoring the church there, Hardy met Emma Lavinia Gifford, sister-in-law of the church's rector. They were married four years later. Much of Hardy's love poetry may have been coloured by the uneven relationship the two shared for over forty years.

6 *Sir Leslie Stephen*. In 1872 Hardy received a letter from Sir Leslie Stephen, one of the literary doyens of the Victorian Age, as a result of seeing his (Hardy's) novel *Under the Greenwood Tree* which had appeared in June. Stephen's encouragement led to Hardy's final abandonment of architecture for novel-writing. Nationwide reputation and success followed, beginning two years later with the outstanding popular success of *Far from the Madding Crowd*.

7 *Max Gate*. After several peripatetic years in London and Dorset, Thomas and Emma Hardy moved to Max Gate, Dorchester (a house designed by Hardy himself) in June 1885. They stayed there for the rest of their lives.

8 *The* Jude *episode*. After several more successful novels, and some less so, in 1895 Hardy published *Jude the Obscure*, his last novel. It created a scandal, was dismissed by numerous leading critics as disgraceful and even obscene, and coincided with his turn to poetry rather than the novel as his literary form from then on. How far the one event caused the other has led to much scholarly speculation.

9 *The two Florences*. In 1893 Hardy and Emma met Florence

Henniker, a married woman, who became friend and cor-
respondent of the poet for thirty years. Probably in 1905
through Florence Henniker he also met Florence Dugdale, an
unmarried woman forty years younger than himself. In 1906
Florence Dugdale became in effect a secretarial and research
assistant to Hardy and in February 1914 his second wife. It is
doubtful whether Hardy was maritally unfaithful with either
of these women, yet they were a main (not total) reason for
the increasing unhappiness of his own marriage.

10 *Death of Emma Hardy*. Suddenly and unexpectedly, late in
1912, Emma Hardy died. A major result was the writing of
the group of poems entitled *Poems 1912–13*.

11 *The final years*. In 1914 the First World War broke out. The
event marked a final hiatus in Hardy's life, as in that of
thousands of others. From 1920 to 1925 there was an attach-
ment, not serious but embarrassing for Florence, to Gertrude
Bugler, an actress sixty years Hardy's junior. Hardy received
countless renowned visitors at Max Gate in this period. In
1910 he had been awarded the Order of Merit, and honorary
Doctorates of Literature came from Cambridge in 1913 and
Oxford in 1920. Hardy died, aged eighty-eight, in 1928.

In 1898 was published *Wessex Poems*, Hardy's first col-
lection of verse. Eight more followed at roughly three-year
intervals, including *Satires of Circumstance* (containing *Poems
1912–13*) in 1914 and *Moments of Vision* in 1917. Finally
came *Winter Words*, published soon after his death.

Now to put some flesh on the bones of this somewhat mechanical list. Since Hardy's father was mason and bricklayer, and
Hardy began his adult life as a professional architect, it is convenient to begin there. We should remember that Hardy, and his
second wife after he died, destroyed much material in the way of
letters, diaries and notebooks, so that we can't always be sure of
detail of a more personal kind.

Thomas Hardy was only just sixteen when, in 1856, he was
apprenticed to the country architect John Hicks in Dorchester.
Late in life he said he wished he had remained a small-town
architect himself;[4] yet his determination, in 1862 aged 22, to go to
London points to the restless temperament that was emerging.
After a few weeks in Kilburn he entered the office of an up-market
architect, Arthur Blomfield, drawing designs and restorations. In
the early 1860s he won various architectural prizes, including one
presented to him by George Gilbert Scott, designer of, among other
buildings, the Houses of Parliament. Hardy was a highly com-

petent draughtsman (his architectural notebook survives) and visited numerous galleries and art exhibitions in his London period. Commissions followed, including a number in the west country and the one at St Juliot's when he met Emma Gifford.

The 1860s was the high period of the Gothic revival in England, and Hardy was extremely sensitive to it. Yet he gave up architecture. Why? He had no antipathy to the profession; rather, the mental restlessness grew which had various strands and which throw light on his emergence as novelist and, later, poet. As we have said, Hardy was brought up a strict Anglican. His faith in conventional terms gradually lapsed in early and middle adult life, but his need for satisfying religious truth in a scientific world, and – differently – his own 'churchiness' (his own word for it), his love of the atmosphere of the church, music, liturgy, Bible and most particularly the Old Testament – these all survived. This 'churchiness' comes out in several poems. 'The Oxen' (p. 229), 'The Clock-Winder' (p. 138), 'The Impercipient' (p. 228), 'To My Father's Violin', (p. 67) 'The Children and Sir Nameless' (p. 179) and 'A Church Romance' (p. 60) and others illustrate the point generally. Hardy always recalled architecture gratefully in later years. One poem in particular, 'The Abbey-Mason' (p. 130), gives an interesting insight into Hardy's poetry generally.

An important name here is that of the Victorian art and architectural critic, John Ruskin. Hardy read much of Ruskin including, probably in 1910, the greatly influential essay 'The Nature of Gothic'[5] in his book *The Stones of Venice* (1851–1853). The next year Hardy toured the cathedrals of England, including Gloucester, where he saw for himself the extraordinary massive diagonal stone beam cutting right across a Gothic screen structure on the south side of the transept. It is widely held to be the earliest example surviving of English Gothic perpendicular, and Hardy's poem 'The Abbey-Mason' is an imaginary story of how a single mason discovered the style. The mason had reached a frustrating point at which he couldn't find the inspiration to bring his designs to resolution. Then, one morning, he saw his drawing-board scored with the icy drops of overnight rain, in such a way that the design he had all along sought was miraculously found.

The poem is one of Hardy's longest 'shorter' poems; about seven pages in our text. It was written furthermore nearly forty years after Hardy had given up architecture, and was dedicated to his first mentor, the Dorchester architect John Hicks. Evidently then architecture as an art and a form had remained with the novelist and poet, deep in his mind. This too is characteristic

of Hardy. In another context, he once said that an incident or
memory would often be exhumed by him as much as thirty or
forty years after it had occurred, and be there ripe for poetic
transformation.[6] But, most of all, I think the point lies in Ruskin's
essay.

As you read more and more of Hardy's poems, you may
begin to wonder just what sort of edifice the whole body, or *oeuvre*
as it is called, amounts to. 'Gothic' seems a good word to describe
it. The great Gothic cathedrals were designed by a few but built
and executed by many. Hundreds of minor masons were allowed
the freedom to make those numerous variations, grotesque
animals, tiny flowers, craggy northern stone which to us is so
familiar. Hardy's work, it is not fanciful to suggest, is of this
nature. He repeatedly devises a new poetic form, takes a new
fleeting incident, sees a curious, sad, perplexing angle on human
affairs. It has an underlying monotony but, as Ruskin put it, is
'capable of perpetual novelty'. Furthermore, Gothic is imperfect;
that is in its nature. Hardy greatly valued, and constantly emphasized, the imperfect in art. He said that poetry must be made
of what is ugly, of nature's defects. He even said, as we quoted
earlier, that the secret of a successful style lay in 'being, in fact, a
little careless, or rather seeming to be ... It brings wonderful life
into the writing'.[7] This sounds very like Gothic itself. But this
seems to contrast with a parallel theme in a different line of
nineteenth-century poets and writers, such as William Wordsworth, Matthew Arnold and John Stuart Mill. Hardy then is
reacting consciously to another currently held nineteenth-century
position, as well as stating his own. Does all this throw light, do
you think, on those oddities of language we noted in Chapter 1?

This liking for imperfection may be significant in a different
area of Hardy's life. As an architect Hardy started in London.
Early on, according to Robert Gittings (*Young Thomas Hardy*,
pp. 89–93: Millgate is more ambivalent) there were signs of a
morbid fascination with the downside of life in London's murkier
parts, as well as the endless interest in women: so often, in
Millgate's words, 'only briefly glimpsed or slightly known'.[8]
(One day in London years later, when he was nearly fifty, Hardy
noticed a young woman on a bus. He noted that she had 'one of
those faces of marvellous beauty which are seen casually in the
streets but never among one's friends ... Where do these women
come from? Who marries them? Who knows them?'.[9]) These
aspects were not unconnected in Hardy's case. The coincidence of
great female beauty in lowly surroundings seems to have struck an
imaginative chord. Hardy probably did not have extramarital

liaisons, but he certainly had many relationships with girls and women in his youth in Dorchester.

There were also two pairs of sisters. One pair, Martha and Tryphena Sparks, were first cousins. It is curious that Hardy had some sort of flirtation with both, even though Martha was six years older than himself while Tryphena was no less than eleven years younger. The Tryphena affair has turned out the more important. When Hardy went back to Dorset as an architect in 1867 Tryphena was sixteen, and Hardy struck up some kind of intimacy with her. The gossip had it that Tryphena bore Hardy an illegitimate child in 1868; more alarmingly, that Tryphena was not his cousin but his niece. Gittings has an appendix demolishing these fantasies,[10] yet the pair were formally engaged at one point and several of Hardy's love-poems are plausibly about Tryphena, notably 'Thoughts of Phena' (p. 327), also written after her death. The other sisters were Eliza and Jane Nicholls, daughters of a Dorset coastguard. Hardy was close to marital engagement with Eliza when he knew her in London in the mid-1860s. But again the other sister figures too, for the engagement with Eliza faltered because Hardy became infatuated with Jane.

Martha Sparks, we noted, was six years older than Hardy, and she wasn't the only one who was older. Yet Hardy's pre-dilections went the other way too. His second wife was forty years his junior; he was also infatuated in old age by the young Gertrude Bugler as we have said. There were others. Elizabeth Bishop was a gamekeeper's daughter in Hardy's home village. Louisa Harding was a farmer's daughter in the same area. Fanny Hurden (the 'poor Fanny Hurd' of 'Voices of Things Growing in a Churchyard', p. 77), was a fellow pupil at the village school. Strangely, Hardy wrote poems to these young girls often as much as fifty years later, on hearing of their deaths, despite not having seen them in all the intervening time. Considering too that Tryphena Sparks was eleven years younger than himself, it seems that young, old and peer were all within the range of his emotions. When Hardy met Emma in 1870 he was already engaged to – well, who? Tryphena Sparks, Eliza and Jane Nicholls and one Cassie Pole have all been suggested. What needs to be remembered in reading the poetry is simply Hardy's tendency to fall for any woman who attracted him, yet with little fruition or result. This would often be because of the woman's resistance – Florence Henniker most notably – and, more generally, one senses how much Hardy was attracted to exactly what he could not have.

These considerations also help introduce the other theme we mentioned earlier in this chapter, namely Hardy's tendency –

perhaps fascination and revulsion combined – toward the morbid, the illicit and seamy side of London life. According to Gittings these tendencies predominated when Hardy was young. Much may have been the natural curiosity of a protected young person over what society saw as the unmentionable sides of sex and loose living. Which of us hasn't felt it? Gittings refers to bantering talk about prostitutes, scandals, political sensation and the like in the architect's office where Hardy worked; less than reverent attention to the Gothic restoration work they were engaged on (no doubt disturbing to our correct churchgoer); and a boastful frequenting of dance-halls and taverns regardless of their rank and reputation.[11]

The poem 'Reminiscences of a Dancing Man' (p. 97) is surely autobiographical on Hardy's part. Hardy may well not have sought sexual satisfaction specifically; rather he was fascinated with the entire atmosphere, the gas-lamps in the fog, the gloom, the compulsively morbid poverty and depravity. This tendency is underlined by the occasions when, still an adolescent in the country, he had gone to some trouble to witness public hangings. In one case he watched distantly from a hillside through a telescope; in the other the condemned prisoner, a woman, swung gruesomely to sado/erotic effect which Hardy still found disturbing years later. The poet's graveyard preoccupations, his skeletons and ghosts, need to be seen if tentatively in this light. It isn't that they themselves are gruesome in their detail; indeed Hardy seldom describes them. But if you were asked whether the kind of preoccupation suggested by such poems was 'healthy' how would you answer? Is such poetry a lancing of such obsessions? You may feel either way on this, and certainly needn't decide now. But much of the world's most powerful literature – including for example Greek tragedy, which Hardy taught himself and greatly respected – is commonly saturated with such events. The tragic suicide in 1873 in Cambridge of a childhood and close lasting friend, Horace Moule, hardly helped the poet to a more cheerful or positive attitude. (The subtitle of the poem 'Standing by the Mantlepiece', p. 287, is 'HMM 1873'.)

We must turn to the formal side of Hardy's career, which grew from the late 1860s. For a long time Hardy had considered the church as a vocation, intending to combine this with writing. The changeover from architecture came with the letter in 1872 from Sir Leslie Stephen, then editor of the highly influential journal *Cornhill Magazine*, for earlier the same year Hardy had felt he had reached the moment of decision. Stephen's offer to serialize Hardy's next novel was a major advance for Hardy. But only ten years later, with the final return of Thomas and Emma to

Dorset in 1881 and Max Gate itself in 1885, did the later run of major novels begin to appear: *The Woodlanders*, *The Mayor of Casterbridge*, *Tess of the d'Urbervilles* (commonly thought of as his masterpiece) and *Jude the Obscure* last of all.

Hardy always found writing in London difficult. He equally found his relationship with Emma increasingly strained, not least because of the embarrassment she is said to have caused him and others by her actions on several public occasions, dinner parties and the like. So despite enjoying being a literary lion in London life, the return to his home county of Dorset, where the great majority of his poetry was written, was perhaps inevitable.

One must also consider how far Hardy's self-inflicted programme of private reading informed and infiltrated his poetry. Hardy had little formal education, and he went to great lengths to rectify this from youth on. He spent much time on the social meliorists of the era, such as Herbert Spencer, Auguste Comte, Charles Darwin and John Stuart Mill. Social amelioration (discussed further in Chapter 7) roughly speaking was the view that human progress could now be achieved not by more or less strict enactment of biblical and church injunctions, but by applying the new natural sciences to material improvement. Hand in hand with this social meliorism for Hardy, therefore, went his increasing religious agnosticism, a problem he shared with numerous Victorian poets and intellectuals, perhaps most famously Tennyson in his long mid-century poem *In Memoriam A.H.H.*. It is not always clear just what Hardy did believe, but he did repeatedly distance himself from fixed religious doctrine, and this comes out in a number of poems which present God, or Nature (personified) as themselves in doubt as to what they have done in making the world. 'God's Funeral' (p. 230), 'Aquae Sulis' (p. 233), 'The Mother Mourns' (p. 243) and 'Nature's Questioning' (p. 288) are among the poems that suggest this, while poems like 'The Oxen' and 'The Impercipient' present doubt as felt by Hardy himself. Some of these poems will be discussed in our final chapters. Thus improvement was, certainly, to be judged in more or less traditional terms, but largely on a general front – a sense of the central importance of love, compassion, tolerance, and most particularly relief of the poor.

When, and why, did Hardy make the decision to switch from novels to poetry? An American Hardy specialist, William Morgan, has investigated the matter closely.[12] Morgan reckons that about a hundred of Hardy's thousand-plus poems can be dated. About thirty-five come from the 1860s, but then only twelve that can be confidently attributed to the next two decades together. The number then rises sharply again, for over forty were then written certainly in the 1890s. The evidence is necessarily of limited value, but it does give a sharp profile on what may have happened.

The novel *Tess of the d'Urbervilles* appeared late in 1891. Its reception was clearly favourable; even the attacks, and there were some, were specifically, if strongly, on certain moral matters or theological statement. Tess's sexuality was held to be too much emphasized, and God depicted as a fiend. Some thought the book drearily written. But these views came from a tiny minority, and as a result of the novel's success Hardy felt able to write the controversial *Jude the Obscure* in, perhaps, a risk-taking frame of mind. The book's reception, according to Hardy, 'cured me of novel-writing for ever', but he had already said as a result of one adverse review of *Tess* that 'if this sort of thing continues no more novel-writing for me. A man must be a fool to deliberately stand up to be shot at'.[13] The supposed fault of *Jude the Obscure* was unorthodoxy on the question of marriage and degeneracy all round. One review was entitled 'Jude the Obscene'. The book was publically burnt by a Church of England bishop, but as Hardy said, books have been burnt throughout history. Certainly Hardy's novels were increasingly becoming vehicles of personal attitudes of his own. It was probably this tendency that made Hardy attack Victorian society more openly, but also made him feel poetry was a more appropriate and tactful medium. In a written communication in 1896 Hardy said that poetry can express unorthodox ideas without getting more than a strange look. Prose sounds more as though the writer meant it, and so may offend more.

He also put the matter more idealistically. In 1888 he had written to a friend Sir George Douglas that 'it is better to fail in poetry than succeed in prose', and in later years he purportedly recalled that 'a sense of the truth of poetry, of its supreme place in literature, had awakened itself in me. At the risk of ruining all my worldly prospects I dabbled in it'.[14] Perhaps he was beginning to find that what he wanted to say was more poetic, or at least more lyrical and inward in nature.

Finally, there were practical considerations. Hardy had financial security now, from his novels and short stories, the collected editions and the magazine serializations; that indeed was his aim in choosing to write novels in the first place. Gittings has also argued[15] that Emma was so angered by the response to *Jude* that Hardy could no longer count on her as a secretary and scribe. Novels are long things; Hardy was getting older, his sight weakening. Practical aspects cannot be ignored.

Hardy's late change to poetry is of more than merely a scholar's interest. When you read the poems, you may gradually form an opinion about Hardy's frequent recallings of long-past events and dead friends, and his speaking in the voice of the dead, rather as though life was already over. It is almost as though Hardy *needed* to wait for later life, and his own poetic imagination could only function in such a context. Perhaps architecture, natural science, and the nineteenth-century realistic novel all needed to be absorbed into his bloodstream before poetic transformation could occur. In later years he himself pointed to the great age of some of the major poets of the ancient world, Homer and Sophocles notably (the latter wrote *Oedipus Rex* when he was ninety). The onset of the First World War only served to distance the past further.

It remains to touch briefly on Hardy's marriage to Emma Lavinia Gifford, his first wife. Hardy had met her, quite by chance, in Cornwall in the spring of 1870 when on an architectural commission. He stayed for four days, walked with her on the cliffs and watched her ride on the Cornish sands by the sea. They married four years later. They seem to have been reasonably happy in the early and middle years, the two years at Sturminster Newton in Dorset from 1876 to 1878 most of all. 'Overlooking the River Stour' (p. 346), which we read in Chapter 1, was written there.

Difficulties probably began with the return from Dorset to Tooting in London, when Hardy felt he needed to be nearer the centre of things. Emma's social ineptitude, her out-of-place remarks and her inappropriate clothes, began to be noticed. Such events continued even after the Hardys returned finally to Dorset and Max Gate, for visits to London's literary world continued. However, it is all too easy to blame Emma. Hardy's social road, despite his own modest social background by the day's standards, was made far easier by his literary status. The years went by. In 1893 the pair met Florence Henniker in Dublin. Ironically the poem 'Alike and Unlike' (p. 358), which evokes his and Emma's very different views of Great Orme's Head off Anglesey, was written only a few days before. Then some time in 1905 or 1906, probably through Florence Henniker, Hardy met Florence Dugdale. These two women in effect came to challenge Emma's place in Hardy's emotional life. By the end of her life Emma's mood was savage. She began to keep hostile and vengeful notebooks about her husband's behaviour and his treatment of her.

Gittings and Millgate both discuss Emma's condition, and Hardy's fear of congenital insanity in her family; the poet's incessant if finally innocent attention to other women; and his own possible lack of sufficient interest in Emma's health. Emma and Thomas didn't meet during the day except at dinner, when they never spoke. On his seventy-second birthday representatives of the Royal Society of Literature came to Max Gate to present the poet with their established award, the society's gold medal for literature. Despite their earnest requests Hardy forbade Emma from attending this ceremony, and she had to leave the room. Who knows where right and wrong lay?

At the end of 1912 Emma died very suddenly of an impacted gall-bladder. How far Hardy knew of her condition already, or should have done, is still the subject of scholarly debate. *Poems 1912–13* (pp. 370–90) was the result. Several were written almost immediately, within weeks and perhaps in some cases days of the event. After Emma's death Hardy wrote to Florence Henniker. He reproaches himself, but a touching passage follows:[16]

> my life is intensely sad to me now without her. The saddest moments of all are when I go into the garden and to that long straight walk at the top that you know, where she used to walk every evening just before dusk, the cat trotting faithfully behind her; & at times when I almost expect to see her as usual coming in from the flower-beds with a little trowel in her hand.

That is almost a Hardy poem itself.[17] A few months later, in the spring of 1913, Hardy took a solitary trip down to St Juliots in Cornwall, where he had met Emma over forty years before. From there he wrote to Florence Dugdale: 'The visit to this neighbourhood has been a very painful one to me, & I have said a dozen times I wish I had not come'.[18] Yet the trip is important for various reasons. A number of the *Poems 1912–13* are set there, and in that past period. And yet, by halfway through the next year he had proposed marriage to Florence Dugdale and she had probably accepted. Since just after Emma's death, Florence had been constantly at Max Gate, causing the gossip in Dorchester as to whether she was Hardy's mistress. They were married early in 1914. But when it was her turn to take on the mantle of being Mrs Thomas Hardy, Florence began to feel growing resentment and perhaps alarm. The number of poems now devoted to Emma in Hardy's later collections made Florence say desperately that the old man was already tired of her. It does seem that a psychic need in Hardy to have the desired object out of reach led him to underestimate the affection needed by those still near him.

Hardy lived for sixteen years after Emma's death. Life took on a more even tenor, and – bar the First World War – there were few if any upheavals or new intellectual incursions from which to draw new material. As a result many poems were written from notes made decades back, or reworked from earlier versions probably equally ancient. The poems become harder to date accurately as the years go by; equally one has to be careful in interpreting their meaning. The poem 'Nobody Comes' (p. 306) was written as late as 1924. It might seem to register despair at the incursion of the modern world. The car (still a recent appearance) 'whangs along in a world of its own', the poet feels that 'It has nothing to do with me'. But Hardy was actually rather fascinated by cars, and this poem was written after he had waited up one night for the return home of a chauffeur-driven car from London, containing his brother and sister, a project in which he had shown much busy enthusiasm. The same applies to numerous Hardy poems.

As the final years went by the stream of eminent literary visitors to the house grew; Hardy seemed happy. Florence was in poor health and her spirits declined steadily. Yet Hardy's poetry and life are not all marital misery and unrequited love. The later period itself shows continued interest in the changing world, its technology, demographic make-up, literary successes, wars and political action. He wrote retrospective poems like 'He Never Expected Much' (p. 309) and 'Afterwards' (p. 304). He wrote war poems, and poems of social and political comment.

When he died, his heart was buried in Stinsford churchyard near his home, and the rest of his cremated body in Westminster Abbey. This divided man had thereby found a fitting symbol, fitting perhaps too in the degree of unwilling attention we must give its details. His duality of perception, toward the planet, women, human artefacts, philosophical ideas and physical objects, never ceased. One of his most famous poems, 'Afterwards', was placed last in *Moments of Vision*. It suggests an anxiety on his part about his perceptive powers, as though in the end that mattered to him most as the basis of his literary art. Listing the objects around him he wonders, in each stanza, 'will the neighbours say,/'He was a man who used to notice such things?'. We raised this matter at the start of the first chapter, and return to it now.

3. Seeing

Having had a quick first look at some poems in Chapter 1, and then sketched the poet's life in Chapter 2, we shall now begin to look much more closely at individual poems. This will be done according to the four themes or areas of Hardy's writing suggested in chapter one – *seeing, love, death* and *language* – and each of these will take one chapter. Before doing so, let me tell you how I propose to go about our discussions in these four chapters.

First, the reminder once again that Thomas Hardy wrote a very large number of poems and that we have, of necessity, to cite quite a good few of them to get any real sense of what he is about. This means that you probably won't be able to look closely at all the ones I am suggesting, and that is quite understandable. But second, then, we must therefore be clear at all times whether we are to read a poem carefully now, or are just alluding to it for some special reason in passing. Some of these latter poems *will* be read in greater detail in later chapters, and I will try to be sure to tell you each time it happens. Third, there are the poems we have read already in Chapter 1. I hope by now you have read all the poems we looked at and dwelt on briefly there (there were about ten or so like that), and perhaps a few more; but you needn't feel you should have studied them in the fullest detail. By now you should, however, be able to recognize the broad aspects of them that this and later chapters will refer to.

In general, may I say I hope you will also build up some kind of instinct for which poems, whether highlighted in this book or just mentioned in passing, are the ones you personally find it useful to home in on. This I know may take time to develop, but again it is important with a poet as prolific as Hardy was. Remember that even David Wright's selection of over three hundred poems is still less than a third of Hardy's whole output! I can really only say: read as many as possible: take your time: and good luck to you. I hope you are also finding a few of your own which I haven't mentioned, for that is always a guarantee of being sure to remember them – not to mention the special excitement of making one's own discoveries.

Please now begin by reading the poem 'On the Departure Platform' (p. 364). It is I think a useful poem with which to start our discussion, even though its very extremity, on this front, makes it untypical. Normally I will ask you to find each poem in the Penguin text. Clearly we can't quote them all, and the habit of becoming familiar with the text itself is a good one. But as an opening orientation let us quote this poem in full:

> We kissed at the barrier; and passing through
> She left me, and moment by moment got
> Smaller and smaller, until to my view
>   She was but a spot;
>
> A wee white spot of muslin fluff
> That down the diminishing platform bore
> Through hustling crowds of gentle and rough
>   To the carriage door.
>
> Under the lamplight's fitful glowers,
> Behind dark groups from far and near,
> Whose interests were apart from ours,
>   She would disappear,
>
> Then show again, till I ceased to see
> That flexible form, that nebulous white;
> And she who was more than my life to me
>   Had vanished quite . . .
>
> We have penned new plans since that fair fond day,
> And in season she will appear again –
> Perhaps in the same soft white array –
>   But never as then!
>
> ' – And why, young man, must eternally fly
> A joy you'll repeat, if you love her well?'
> – O friend, nought happens twice thus; why,
>   I cannot tell!

Here are some questions about it:

1 How many words can you find concerning eyesight?
2 What do you end up knowing about the lady?
3 How are the last two stanzas different from the first four?
4 Have you had an experience like this yourself?

DISCUSSION

I count five 'eyesight' words, but it depends just what you do count. 'A wee white spot of muslin fluff', for example, is strongly visual. But in general, it seems to me that this poem conveys physical eyesight more sharply and exclusively than any other does. Almost unalloyed, it gives central place to seeing itself.

What is clear surely is how deeply Hardy feels the lady's presence through the one mode. It is not the tone of her voice, the touch of her body when he kissed her, or even any expression on her face. He sees her so clearly, yet we don't even know if she was smiling, let alone any memories of the meeting just ending. It is the fact, stripped down to that only, that he can see her and then he can't, and how that diminishing optical view happens, that holds him. Only in that context does he briefly relate any human matter, such as the other travellers 'Whose interests were apart from ours', or that the lady 'was more than my life to me'. I imagine that most people have had this visual experience, of saying goodbye to someone at platform or airport, and seeing them getting further and further away while increasingly disappearing and reappearing, the disappearances getting longer, the quick sightings briefer. The first four stanzas are so vivid about this that one is whimsically tempted to reverse the film ('On the Arrival Platform' perhaps) ending presumably with the kiss and rather different concluding thoughts. The prominence of eyesight is found all over Hardy, and many of the poems have this explicitness on the matter.

But we then see that in 'On the Departure Platform' the last two stanzas begin to ask questions and widen the implication. It is still visual; the poet hopes his love will 'appear' again perhaps even identically dressed. But, he sadly feels, it will never be the same again, and furthermore this is for no more specific reason than that nothing ever is; 'nought happens twice'. And he doesn't even know why *that* is; 'Why,/I cannot tell!'. And the poem ends. So one is left wondering about such laser-like observation of every detail of her shrinking departure. What has been the advantage of expressing it? In his novel *The Unbearable Lightness Of Being* the Czech novelist Milan Kundera wrote: 'What happens but once, says the German adage, might as well not have happened at all.' Is this the view this poem ends up with?

In 'On the Departure Platform' there is a strong suggestion that camera-like accuracy is not the whole truth about eyesight in human terms. We will say more about the camera – still a recent invention after all in Hardy's time – in Chapter 7. We shall glance there at poems like 'The Photograph' (p. 326) and 'Thoughts of Phena' (p. 327), and consider how far there the camera's preservation of human life is found to be inadequate. But literally dozens of Hardy's poems depend on the matter of

direct vision. Sometimes the titles convey that interest, as with
'The Blinded Bird' (p. 220), 'The Impercipient' (p. 228), 'She Who
Saw Not' (p. 366) and 'The Glimpse' (p. 165). These are among
the poems you needn't read now, but please notice their titles.
These all seem to convey *failure* to see, rather than just seeing, as
though that lack worries the poet somewhat. But more generally,
what matters is that 'seeing' itself is made explicit. There are also
numerous poems in which seeing is made explicit in the first line
or very soon afterwards. Again there is no need to read these now,
and I will not assume that you have done so, but you might care
to choose one or two at random for your own interest. Such first-
line examples include 'We are getting to the end of visioning' ('We
are getting to the end', p. 287), 'I saw a slowly-stepping train'
('God's Funeral', p. 230), 'From here, the quay, one looks above
to mark' ('The Harbour Bridge', p. 175), ' "What do you see in
that time-touched stone?" ' ('In the British Museum', p. 169), 'I
have seen her in gowns the brightest' ('The Old Gown', p. 334)
and finally here 'When I look forth at dawning, pool', the opening
line of 'Nature's Questioning' (p. 288), a crucial poem on this
subject to which we shall return later in this chapter. And dozens
of poems, while not naming sight as such, clearly set a scene at the
very outset, like 'Snow in the Suburbs' (p. 225) as we saw in
Chapter 1. Others are clearly visual throughout even when they
don't say so explicitly. You can look for further examples yourself
of all these kinds – you won't find it hard to spot them, and
opening the poems anywhere brings them up very quickly. Such
examples occur in the novels too.[1]

Now let's look at a poem more closely again. This next poem,
'The Darkling Thrush' (p. 218), 'sees' a little differently, and you
may wonder at first how far it comes into this chapter's category. I
would ask two questions here. **First, how does the level of detail
compare here with that in 'On the Departure Platform'? Second,
what do you make of the 'voice' that comes in halfway through,
at the start of stanza three?** Please consider carefully your own
answers to these questions before reading the discussion that
follows.

DISCUSSION

My own view is that the platform poem emphasizes eyesight
excessively but surface-wise, while this poem, 'The Darkling
Thrush', refers to it less but, in the end, more deeply. The first
stanza might seem to paint, or at least suggest, the scene straight-
forwardly enough, viewed from the 'coppice gate' the poet is

leaning on. Clearly – indeed quite undeniably – he is out of doors in the twilight and can see the trees, wintry land, sky and so on. But can he? Or, at least, does he really say so? Apart from the 'tangled bine-stems' (strictly hops or vines but allowably any high creeping plant) there is no detail at all. There is nothing in the first two stanzas, which are half the poem, apart from the bine-stems and, rather oddly it now turns out, the land's 'sharp features'.

It could be that the twilight details are clear to the poet but that he is not passing them on to us. But why then would he want to say so? Well, we may answer, he is simply evoking a mood of sadness and past time, and here one should note the famous date at the end of this famous Hardy poem, giving edge to the phrase 'The Century's corpse outleant'. But I notice then how the second half of the poem changes from the first. We switch from sight to sound, and suddenly and surprisingly at the start of stanza three, 'At once a voice arose . . .'. And we then learn that this is the call of the thrush 'In a full-hearted evensong', whose joyfulness in voice it seems contrasts the 'gloom' (such a common Hardy word) the eye must perceive.

There is much that could be said about this, and we can only touch some of it briefly. This 'gloom' of Hardy's, which you will find in many poems, is a word for the greyness that his poems exude nearly always. As said in Chapter 1, very few of Hardy's poems are brightly coloured. This mind-coloured poetry reflects or expresses Hardy's interest in 'neutral-tinted haps' (i.e. happenings), a phrase he used in a late career-summarizing poem 'He Never Expected Much' (p. 309). Doubtless when writing that he also recalled the title of one of his very earliest poems, 'Neutral Tones' (p. 55), where a similar idea is expressed. For many readers, however, this aspect will also recall by contrast Shelley's famous lines in 'Adonais': 'Life, like a dome of many-coloured glass/Stains the white radiance of Eternity', which is exactly what Hardy's poetry does not. In context of 'The Darkling Thrush' we should, again briefly, mention here the echo of the Romantic poet's 'To a Skylark', which this poem too echoes but contrasts. For Shelley the lark's ecstatic song is an uplift for the poet himself. The natural world could be seen straight on, and admired and loved for that reason. But for Hardy, the thrush's optimistic song, also in the 'ecstatic' tones of Shelley ('. . . carolings/Of such ecstatic sound') have 'little cause'. And we will consider later how far this seeing in Hardy but in grey, in gloom, is itself an expression of a late nineteenth-century reaction to Romantic optimism.

But as we have said already, in 'The Darkling Thrush' there is also this clear switch from sight to sound. The thrush itself is 'darkling', an obscure word with little widespread use. In an earlier, famous and pessimistic poem, 'Dover Beach', Matthew Arnold had written that 'we' (i.e. in effect the Victorian age) 'are here as on a darkling plain.../Where ignorant armies clash by night'. To cut the point short, the various connotations of 'darkening', 'getting darker' and the like seem to hang around, if not so much the thrush itself, more here the evening twilight where this darkling or dimly-seen thrush starts singing, very loudly.

This switch from sight to sound happens in a number of Hardy's poems. In one sense it did in 'On the Departure Platform', in that a voice as of a friend comes in to ask the poet the import of his experience. 'The Harbour Bridge' contains such a switch, and 'On Sturminster Foot-Bridge' (p. 348), so visual in itself, carries the sub-title '(Onomatopoeic)', a fact which escaped some of Hardy's reviewers. The sight-sound emphasis is even more marked in the three poems 'She Who Saw Not', 'At Lulworth Cove a Century Back' (p. 214) and 'In the British Museum' (p. 169). Each contains an alternate voice to that of the poet, which questions him about his visual experience and, what is more interesting, some third person or presence as well. However, my suggestion is that in all these eyesight poems, including the ones discussed earlier, eyesight's inadequacy along with its necessity are somehow at odds with each other. The poet finds himself looking; this comes in many poems. Yet when he looks, it is in gloom, perhaps in two senses, and other senses (in another sense!), such as voice, enter the picture. We will come to wider speculations about what this could have meant in the historical situation of the time, its technological innovations, religious doubts and political ideologies.

Here first though is a further mode by which 'seeing' is itself seen and poetically handled. There are a whole set of poems which refer to *lamps, mirrors, artificial gas-light* and *windows*. All of these are clearly things which in some way support or adapt eyesight, or make it more useful. The artificiality of these things should not be overstressed perhaps, for so often with Hardy, even 'indoors', one senses a landscape and elements not far away. The setting is seldom as wholly man-made as in 'On the Departure Platform'; more often the windows will look out on trees and fields and rain, and the lamps are likely to be in a foggy lane or by a river. Rather we will wonder whether the presence of a window or a light in some way even curtails perception, or attempts vainly to enhance it.

Let's look at such a poem now. I suggest 'On the Esplanade',

which you will find on page 323 of our text and which I would
now ask you to read.

   Is this a lamp poem or a window poem? How successful is
the poet's description of the sea, and why does he so elaborate it?
Why, in contrast, does he want to emphasize what he does 'not
know' in the last line of all three stanzas? And what is it that Fate
is creeping up with?

DISCUSSION

The poem has three stanzas. The first two both seem to be de-
scribing the sea at night, from the promenade in a small town
resort (it was in fact Weymouth). The last line of each of these
stanzas says that 'all' this is 'plain' to the poet but that there is
something else he doesn't know. In the third stanza the poet turns
to an open window in a house by the sea. Through it in the room
inside there is 'unseen' – so this time he hears her – a woman
playing an instrument and singing. Yet this too the poet 'marked',
just as the seascape had been 'plain'; but the sudden reflection at
the very end is the fact 'That, behind,/My Fate's masked face crept
near me I did not know!'

   At least one critic, Rosemary Sumner, has suggested that, as
in the first part of 'The Darkling Thrush', the sea is in fact not
described in any precise visible detail, even though we still end up
feeling we have seen it.[2] Of course, a recognizable light is cast,
and the result is compelling, with the 'tumbling twinkle of shines'
(the way wave-crests catch the moon), the 'constant mile of curve'
of the bay; the 'pearl-strung row' of lamps and their 'gimlets of
light'. What you think of Sumner's view may well have some
bearing on how the poem strikes you as a whole. The distinction
is clearly made between the poet's seeing the night-time seascape
(including its lamps) while only hearing the woman in the room,
yet in both cases he seems to feel he does see/hear what is there. I
sense a touch of guilty voyeurism lurking in the poem, to be
punished by Fate's appropriately apt intervention. I also feel that
the 'Fate' must itself be some event in the realm of love, but
cannot be sure how far this is because I know how much Hardy
wrote on that topic. But finally, we might notice that an ironic
doubling-up has occurred. Just as the woman in the room doesn't
know the poet is there, so too the poet can't know that his own
fate, in certainly different form, is creeping up behind him, and in
this case with greater effect. Now if something of all this is a fair
reading, then the visible aspect of the night sea, which makes the
poem's backcloth, is important in standing in for what *either* we

do clearly see, but to no avail, *or* yet again something we see but only in part, only as an impression. Hardy's sea scene is certainly touched in by much the 'impressionistic' way of the art movement of that name and of his time; surfaces matter, and solidity is shown in touches of light.

So I think that 'On the Esplanade' touches on nescience, on not-knowing, in a special way, and with more elaboration than usual. But I think too that the 'window' is partly symbolic of what may both aid and block our seeing and so our knowing. The window lets us see in, but the watcher is still outside and kept there. There are many poems which include lamps, gaslight or mirrors, which you might consider in your own time. They include 'We Sat at the Window' (p. 344), 'Seen by the Waits' (p. 95), 'Beyond the Last Lamp' (p. 167), 'An August Midnight' (p. 215), 'In Church' (p. 121) and 'The Convergence of the Twain' (p. 277).

But we must now take this discussion a stage further. For hitherto we have still tended to look at the cases where 'seeing' or its opposite are quite closely related to the optical act. But let me ask a question here. From the poems you have read thus far, do you find, surprising as it may sound, even a *blindness* at work? Does Hardy not seem to sense an unseeing quality in sight itself? In poems like 'The Darkling Thrush' and 'A Light Snow-Fall after Frost' (p. 168), was it that the more you peer into the gloom the more you were aware of the sad impossibility of perception? And is it equally that the more you think you have seen very clearly and sharply, as in poems like 'Snow in the Suburbs' (p. 225), 'Overlooking the River Stour' (p. 346) or even our first poem here 'On the Departure Platform' itself, the more it turns out that our camera-accuracy either is useless, or really tells us little or nothing?

My feeling is that maybe a two-layered idea of sight is at work, corresponding to our two meanings of the phrase 'I see' as literal or metaphorical. Thus it can mean either, I physically see the yellow car, or the second door on the left; or it can mean 'now I understand'. The second meaning survives in our language today, more commonly as 'I'm with you', 'I'm on your wavelength'. All those emphasize the human relationship rather than the eyesight metaphor. In this respect our orientation today is different from that felt by many in Hardy's time. Thanks to historicist ideologies, social anthropology, psychology itself and a number of other approaches to reality (including a revival of interest in religion) we are more likely today to feel that a whole range of cultural factors participate in our understandings of each other. In Hardy's time purely physical and often biological science

was too recent to be other than overwhelming in its power
to shake established cultural conceptions. In such an obsessively
natural-science milieu of the nineteenth century, post-Darwin,
perceptive people like Hardy were all too conscious of the limitations of our understanding if indeed that really was just an exten-
sion and application of our physical sense of the material world.
There was, to be sure, a continuing tradition of the subjective and
metaphysical, which continued to believe in an essential presence
within each human being, qualitatively of greater worth than that
suggested by neutral analysis of the purely physical, and deriving
ultimately via the creation itself from God. The names of Kant,
Hegel, Coleridge and Newman are associated with such a tradition (there was also the new tradition of 'culture' in the sense of
high civilization and cultivation, associated with Matthew Arnold).
It was exactly such traditions of which Hardy became increasingly
sceptical. As we shall see later this chapter, in examining the poem
'Nature's Questioning', Hardy could see no way past the doubts
science had brought.

So we might expect to find some poems by Hardy where
these wider and deeper extensions seem prevalent. Certainly for
example in 'The Impercipient' and 'The Oxen' (p. 229), which you
can read now or not as you wish, the church building and the
stable respectively are only touched in as background, and so may
be only metaphors for a more spiritual unseeing. (In both poems
Hardy expresses a yearning to believe what orthodox Christians
still believed.) But here I would like to raise in more detail a
further kind of poem; those haunted by ghosts. For when we find
Hardy saying that he can't see the solid material world because of
intruding ghosts, we realise surely that this matter of seeing/not-
seeing is indeed more than a matter of camera-reliability. Hardy it
seems really is wondering now, how much our apprehensions of
the world are reliable, even when they seem sharp, black and
white, lucidly edged (as to tree, field, chair, vase, etc.) in ordinary
eyesight terms. A major spiritual presence in the nineteenth
century was John Henry Newman (1809–1890), whose work
Hardy read and admired. Newman did not believe in ghosts, but
he once asked what our reactions would be if we incontrovertibly
saw a person alive and spoke to them when we had equally
incontrovertibly been present at their death.[3] Did Hardy then feel
the presence of his ghosts more than the real places where he saw
them?

It could be worth reading Hardy's ghost poems in that light.
Try 'Who's in the Next Room?' (p. 303). Then ask yourself:

1 How many people are there in the poem?
2 Do they all exist, or are some imagined? Are any ghosts?
3 Is eyesight the only mode of apprehension? Why does the poet also say 'I seem to hear', 'I seem to feel' as well as 'I seemed to see'?

DISCUSSION

Surely we notice in this poem the presence of, not just the man 'in the next room', but the third voice too, who answers the poet in the last line of each stanza. Who is *that* person? we might also ask. Perhaps we are reminded of the 'third' people in 'At Lulworth Cove a Century Back' or 'In the British Museum'. Furthermore, this mysterious third person seems to agree that the man in the next room does exist. When you ask someone whether you saw a person in the next room, and they answer 'no you didn't – but he was there', it is a bit chilling. 'Nay: you saw nought. He passed invisibly'. And this is continued in the final line of successive stanzas. The poet thinks he heard a voice and felt a breath: the companion presence denies this, but doesn't deny that anyone is there. In fact it seems to affirm it. It is merely that this person in the next room doesn't speak and doesn't even breathe.

It looks rather as though our mysterious third person has special access to knowledge of ghosts, more than Hardy does. But I think it unlikely that this third person is a ghost too. Rather, there may be simply a dramatic presentation by dialogue of a disturbance in Hardy's mind. Yet that doesn't prevent this strange speaker taking a role in the poem's action. And as to the three refrains: 'I seemed to see', but then 'I seem to hear', 'I seem to feel'; the sense is apparently that the ghost presence deflects the poet from 'seeing' as the sole emphasis, for three senses are touched on in the refrain, not just one. The strong suggestion, surely, is that presences human or superhuman are 'felt' – now in a wider sense – rather than just crudely seen or heard or touched, and that this feeling rather limits one's direct eyesight powers. The poet seems to be stumbling about blindly, asking questions, uncertain. If strong eyesight were sufficient that would be unnecessary. So again the suggestion might seem to be that camera accuracy is not enough, or that camera accuracy and spiritual or even fully human seeing are not synonymous, perhaps not compatible.

The late Victorian period was of course the strong period of spiritualism and seances, the point being that 'ghosts' in the everyday sense of some non-fleshed but close-by presence of a dead person, came to seem much needed. If suddenly the belief in an afterlife, where we shall all meet again, evaporates, there comes the anxiety and need to keep one's dear ones near to you. Hence the visits to graveyards where one would kneel and whisper to the loved dead; or the night-time mutterings to whoever shared your bed when they were alive. Hardy was exceptionally aware of these things.

I hope enough has been said by now to alert you to the variety of ways in which failure to see in the very act of doing so seems to pervade this body of poetry. The poem 'Afterwards' (p. 304) is sometimes taken as Hardy's final comment not only on this topic of seeing but on his approach to life more generally. The poet speculates wistfully about how he might be remembered after death, as 'a man who used to notice such things'. I will leave you to examine it for yourself now or later. But meanwhile let us here give detailed attention to one final poem, which in addressing the matter seems to be led by it to deeper, and perhaps sadder, philosophical questions. The poem is 'Nature's Questioning' (p. 288). There are three main questions to ask. **First, what do we make of Hardy's feeling in stanza one, that the objects he sees are also staring at himself? Equally though, how can they see anything at all if, as stanza five says, they are remains of Godhead 'brain and eye now gone'? Finally, if Hardy is 'No answerer' (stanza seven) to these objects' questions, how firm are his affirmations in the poem's last three lines?**

DISCUSSION

The poem does raise the question of eyesight from an extra-ordinary angle.

> When I look forth at dawning, pool,
>   Field, flock, and lonely tree,
>   All seem to gaze at me
> Like chastened children sitting silent in a school;
> Their faces dulled, constrained, and worn . . .

The objects look back at the poet who is himself looking at them. This itself is a remarkable feature of eyesight, and its refusal to be tied down to a matter of objective record, or photograph. What makes one say of someone, a beautiful woman, or a guilty-looking street pedestrian, that they 'know they are being watched'? Yet these objects then begin to speak. They say sadly that they don't

know why they exist or where they came from – a common
Victorian theological doubt of course. But one possible origin they
consider of themselves is this:

> 'Or come we of an Automaton
> Unconscious of our pains? . . .
> Or are we live remains
> Of Godhead dying downwards, brain and eye now gone?'

So they think their eyes have gone. This is surely a clear suggestion
by the poet that the seeing and the unseeing are one and the same
thing, or at least strongly overlap. These objects look back at the
poet, but then wonder if they themselves have eyesight at all.
We might feel perhaps that Hardy is simply projecting his own
feelings onto nature, as the romantic poets did. But the romantic
poets did so far more optimistically. Consider too the word 'gaze'
in stanza one. It is another of Hardy's 'seeing' words, and you will
come across it in other poems. Perhaps I am being fanciful, but I
find it hard to eliminate the rhyming word 'haze' from my mind
when I come across Hardy's 'gaze'. Equally the word 'glaze'
suggests itself, as though the eyes are glazed over in the very act of
perception. Both echoes suggest a limit on perception.

Hardy himself can offer no solace ('no answerer I . . .').
Rather, he elaborates (in the form of questions put by nature's
objects) a set of possible explanations as to how these objects feel
themselves to be so ignorant of what they are and why that makes
them feel 'chastened . . . dulled, constrained, and worn'. They
wonder if God is an imbecile, or an automaton, or indeed dying.
Even their one more positive suggestion in stanza six, that there is
'some high Plan' which nature (and humans) can't know about,
entails the accompanying fear that they themselves must be
walked over ('strides') as the plan unfolds. So the poem turns out
to be true to its title: much is imagined, nothing explained. The
poem is one of Hardy's chief early statements of his general doubt
about this world's apprehensibility by humans, and his more
immediate everyday fear that our ordinary eyesight may betray us
even when it seems most accurate.

Yet the poet is not prevented from powerful imaginative
suggestions: he sees inwardly, whatever else. The notion of
the 'Godhead dying downwards' in stanza five sorts oddly yet
interestingly against the vivid picture of the objects as children –
nineteenth-century children, out of the poorhouse it almost
seems – 'sitting silent in a school' and cowered by the very
oppressiveness which, even so, is mindless itself, an imbecility, an
automaton. The vivid picture of children in school enables us to

take the rather abstract suggestions of the next three stanzas
without losing attention. For they feel like real questions, borne
painfully through suffering, and to answer them would be not
merely important academically but an end to desperation and
hopelessness.

This poem also exemplifies a mode of approach to unseeing
and unknowing that Hardy often employs. It was J. Hillis Miller
who coined the phrase 'double vision' to catch this aspect of
Hardy's visual tendency.[4] Again and again a Hardy poem not only
sees, but sees from two points of view, or sees two contrasting
things one after another, with equal weight given to both, so
that both reader and poet are left uncertain or even bewildered.
Examples from the poems already mentioned include 'Who's in
the Next Room?', 'A Light Snow-Fall after Frost', 'Overlooking
the River Stour', 'In the British Museum', 'On the Esplanade' and
all the sight/sound ones by nature. You might care to check back
to them from time to time. In 'Overlooking the River Stour' for
example the poet stares accurately at the river but forgets to look
at what is behind his back. In 'A Light Snow-Fall after Frost' the
scene is considered before the snowfall and after it, and neither
predominates. In 'Nature's Questioning' the duality is found in the
two perspectives of vision. The objects are the questioners, the
poet is the failed answerer; but equally, we might say, the poet is
questioner, and the objects fail to answer him. The 'double vision'
is, then, another way of suggesting that there can be no reliable
single vision; we cannot know the answers to our questions, or
resolve our sadnesses. The form pervades Hardy's poems, and we
shall find many more examples even when 'seeing' is no longer our
specific topic.

So 'seeing' is troublesome for Hardy, scientifically, philosophically and in human terms. Poetically however, I believe he
transcends the difficulty. For, when all is said, at an everyday level
he still sees quite a lot! Jeremy Hooker, himself a Wessex poet of
considerable achievements, has declared that by virtue of this
quality Hardy 'saw a place as no one has before, and no one
has since'.[5] How then does he manage to leave us with this
poetic satisfaction even when we are no clearer about our human
predicament? I will end by suggesting just one way. We talk
often of a poet or novelist 'telling a story' if they are narrative
writers, but 'painting a scene' if their talent is more descriptive.
In mischievous fashion I will confound these, and talk of 'painting
a story' and 'telling a scene'. Look at the many poems we have
considered. Don't some of them 'tell a scene' – this poem 'Nature's
Questioning' for example, or 'On the Departure Platform' and

'On the Esplanade'? They narrate, but through the poet's visual observations rather than an unfolding tale.

But the reverse happens too. For, despite the many poems we have now opened up in this chapter, none yet has been a full-bodied narrative poem in which the story and its characters dominate. If I dare suggest it, here is just one last poem. It is called 'Life and Death at Sunrise' (p. 57). Couldn't one say this poem 'paints a story'?

4. Love

'Seeing' is of course less a topic than a general characteristic of Hardy's writing. We can now take a specific topic. As David Wright pointed out, many of Hardy's poems are about love and marriage. Indeed, of the poems we have already named on all matters, at least a dozen might well be called love poems, or love-and-marriage poems, of one kind or another, even though I have so far discussed them in some other context.

Let's start by summarizing what we have already said on the matter.

1 In biographies and letters concerning Hardy we read of passing fancies, former loves, missed opportunities, and his own home and marriage. The question arises of how far we should use this material to interpret the poems. You may think they should be able to stand on their own, and I for one would broadly sympathize with that. Difficulties can arise though, because sometimes a piece of biographical information is such as to force a different interpretation upon us. Take for example the short poem 'A Thunderstorm in Town' (p. 358), which we discussed briefly in Chapter 1. It could refer to the companion of an evening with no great involvement, or (as usually suggested) to Mrs Florence Henniker, whom Hardy knew for thirty years and to whom he was unquestionably drawn.

2 *Poems 1912–13*. Many critics, for example Dennis Taylor, see the *Poems 1912–13* as central to the entire body of work, and indeed the place where his restless yet perhaps unreachable desires at last find full expression. (You'll recall from chapter two that these were the poems written soon after the death of Emma Hardy in 1912.) Other critics have disagreed, and we need simply to avoid making assumptions about the sequence's status too early. It is clearly an important sequence.

3 The four love poems we have looked at in any detail so far, 'On the Departure Platform' (p. 364), 'On the Esplanade' (p. 323), 'Faintheart in a Railway Train' (p. 317) and 'A Hurried Meeting' (p. 176), all suggest love in varying degrees of lack. This went from the strange frustration of the first as the loved one disappears, to the explicit idea of love as a 'terrible thing . . . all mourning, mourning' of the last. Is that going to be a keynote? This chapter will work toward answering that question.

I would like now to introduce a few poems for our consideration, one by one, and moving roughly on a line from the poet's seeming detachment to his involvement. We then end with some of the *Poems 1912–13*, presumably the most involved of all. Of course, this is to impose a structure of sorts already, but here and there I will also list further poems, which you can choose among in order to build a fuller picture. First, let's look at what seems a fairly detached poem from the writer's point of view, indeed something of a traditional ballad narrative. This is 'A Trampwoman's Tragedy' (p. 115). This poem was much admired by Ezra Pound and the American writer Ford Maddox Ford; it became rather notorious in the early twentieth century, and for a long period was banned from educational anthologies.[1] Please read this poem now and then answer for yourself the following questions:

1 Do you think the woman narrator behaved shoddily?
2 What do all the details about pubs, walks and scenery add?
3 How soon do we know we are in for a sad ending?
4 What causes the lover's agony in stanza eight? (I can think of two explanations.)

DISCUSSION

Love, jealousy, murder and hanging, set against a clear rural background in just on a hundred lines, this might seem to be a prototype ballad story. And so perhaps it is. Look at how the second line in each stanza half-repeats the first, and the straight run of three rhymes in the second half of each stanza. These seem to take this energized rattling poem forward, as also surely do words like 'jaunted' and 'fancy-man', and the light-hearted bit about being stung by midges and the listing of the best pubs for the ramblers *en route*. The woman speaking even has time, at the end of stanza six, to evaluate the scenery. But since she already knows her story's outcome we may be tempted to wonder how she can feel as she does. Perhaps she is insensitive, or else could be covering over more agonized feelings.

My answer would be that this is the wrong approach. The traditional ballad, which this poem imitates, allows only mythological kinds of meaning, not psychological ones. The speaker is surely to be taken as a prototype figure who accepts a way of life which does not allow much inquiry and whose changes and chances must be borne as they come. This is why the speaker can respond to these details about walks and pubs and landscape, and then switch without awkwardness to the tragic outcome. We know nothing about this woman and do not need to. In a traditional world, jealousy in love is as perennial as the natural setting in which it takes place.

In fact the poet has prepared us for tragedy along the way. There is the odd menacing term – clearly 'jeering John' but then perhaps 'unseen' at the end of the fourth stanza. So when the 'deadly day!' bit comes in stanza five we know we are on the road to a conventional sad/bad ending. The neutrality of the woman narrator is contrasted, furthermore, by the intensity of the real lover who believes himself deceived. The murdered man is different again; he never speaks, bar a brief claim in stanza seven, and offers no I-didn't-mean-no-harm kind of excuse, as he might have. So if you feel – as I do – that stanza eight is the poem's most intense, you may wonder whether this is where the poet puts in feelings he most understands. He is touching on intimate ground. Certainly the Victorian reader would have thought so, which is why the poem was often suppressed, as already said. And finally, the lover's agony in stanza eight can be read two ways. If his 'care' was indeed successful, the child to be born is not his. If it is his child, then his 'care' has failed. But the point here is that that dilemma is itself the poem's point of drama. It is not a matter of the emotional involvement of the poet. As always with a ballad, the singer is detached. A ballad story indeed may have occurred – and often did – centuries before.

The poem then at least feels detached. Now, if at this point we recall 'Faintheart in a Railway Train' (p. 317) and 'On the

Esplanade' (p. 323), we see a slight change. In those poems the
poet himself is just entering the corner of the picture; not affecting
the people he sees and not knowing them, but himself present and
emotionally concerned with them as real. Yet he only sees them
through windows, one of a house, one of a train. Along our
continuum a fraction further still we might place 'A Thunderstorm
in Town'. There the poet himself was inside the hansom cab with
the lady, and the window itself is mentioned as enclosing them
both. I would like to suggest that at this point you mentally range
these few poems in your mind and see whether you agree with the
degree of increasing involvement I have suggested: then please
turn to the fifth poem, which I suggest takes us one degree further
in still.

Please now read the poem 'A Countenance' (p. 352). Bear in
mind this general picture but also, without being too predisposed,
consider what you think of it along the following lines:

1 Is the poet writing of someone he actually met?
2 Does any word stand out for you in this poem more than any
other?
3 How important imaginatively is the physical characteristic to
which he is drawn?
4 What is the poet's mood? Happy, sad, erotic? Do we know
anything about the woman's response?

DISCUSSION

My own feeling is that in this poem the poet is drawn yet a little
nearer to full emotional encounter. This is suggested in two ways.
The line 'Alas! I knew not much of her' seems to imply that he
was at least acquainted (rather than that he saw her once across a
room). Also of course, there is the sweet and obviously magnetic
characteristic of the woman's mouth. I wonder what you think of
this poem. I like its gentle indirection, the things said askance or
merely implied, the way the lulling subdued rhythm suggests this,
and the way the word 'quite' appears at line-ends four times yet
rhymes only with itself; for me it is the poem's key word.

The poem's attitude may not appeal to all readers, perhaps
especially women. It might be called sado-masochistic, or at least
expressive of need for domination. For the laugh 'not in the
middle of her face quite', which the poet it seems loves – the last
line quietly slips this in – is caused by her anxiety; it is shy and
nervous. He is drawn to the physical feature that expresses her

frailty and discomfort. The poet without, so to speak, consulting her, looks one by one at her features, and let his eyes dwell on them; the curls, the lips and the laugh itself. One could call this 'protectiveness'; I wouldn't be convinced. Yet it seems gentle. He associates himself with her inadequacies by poetically parallelling his own: he too 'could not trace quite', the same word putting his incomplete understanding of her on a level with her own lack of confidence. He associates her too with 'Bright sun on midsummer leaves' by what critics sometimes call metonymy; that is to say, he doesn't compare her with them but puts them near her, like a halo or fitting backcloth. And in asking himself the questions at the end, he draws off his intruding power into a wider puzzlement. We don't know why 'love' would become 'unblinded', so that might refer to a general human condition in love, or its likelihood.

Let me leave it with you. You might think the poet's uncertain indirection adequately matches the lady's sidelong smile; but you would then have to wonder whether he 'lost all sight of her' through mere circumstance or because she did not respond herself. But the poet stays open on that matter. We aren't told how she in turn felt about him, and that enables the poet to concentrate, and to concentrate the reader, on the facial characteristic he found so endearing.

Here our continuum, already artificial, becomes complex. For having got as near as this, there are many ways, in other poems, in which the poet may approach the woman, encounter her, remember her, forget her, be shunned by her, despair of her, lack courage to speak to her, and so on. Hardy even speaks in the woman's voice at times, as we saw – rather distantly – in 'A Trampwoman's Tragedy'. But what is important for us now is the increasing presence of the poet as involved rather than detached. The next group of poems I would like to consider illustrates this in an unusual way. In this group the poet seems fully involved emotionally but the loved woman is absent. Perhaps you would now like to read the poem 'The Sunshade' (p. 138). We won't spend a lot of time on it but it does offer a way of considering this question further. Here are some questions for you to answer – again before going on to my own discussion.

1 Is 'The Sunshade' a love poem?
2 I said in Chapter 1 (p. 4) that only a very few of Hardy's poems contain colour. This poem looks like one of them. What part do the colours play?
3 What do you make of 'skeleton', 'ribs' and 'bones'?

DISCUSSION

The poet simply finds an old sunshade on a beach. It is rotted, the
material gone, only the spiky frame surviving, and must have
been lost years before. The poet immediately imagines certain
things about it and its owner. He talks of the sunshade in terms
of skeletons, ribs and the rest, presumably in a straightforward
metaphor for human death. Just as the sunshade has rotted with
the years, so too might its owner have done. The opening of the
last stanza four makes this explicit. But in the third stanza Hardy
has also suggested that the owner might have been thinking about
love herself. There is not the slightest warrant for this belief (nor
does the poet give one); rather, he imagines her 'love-stratagem'
while at the same moment introducing a picture of her own bodily
physique, in the very intriguing and appealing line, her 'Little
thumb standing against its stem'. The little thumb stands in for the
girl herself, making her seem small and demure; and it too, like
the woman in 'A Countenance', seems to need protection, or be
protected, by standing against the sunshade's larger 'stem'.

But since there is also the comparison with death, Hardy
again seems to approach love by having it removed, out of reach.
Here I feel is the significance of the poem's colours. The 'hue of its
dyes', the 'white or pink', appear to stand for the living healthy
desirable woman's flesh, and the sun brought that out. Now, a
skeleton, it is hidden – 'that none may scan', beyond redemption
of the sun's rays which – like Shelley's many-coloured glass –
could be refracted into the colours of the spectrum as parasols
often seem to be, and which originally it absorbed and reflected in
the very act of fending them off from the person it kept cool.
The association of the colours with life is brought out by the
wordplay; the 'livers and diers' (people who live and die) turn into
the 'dyes', or colours, of stanza two. But finally the woman, now
beyond Hardy's reach, is somehow resurrected. The first line of
stanza three suggests the possibility; it is taken back a little in
stanza four, but the ghost of the woman still has regret; that is,
she still feels.

Is this poem, which refers to no woman the poet could
possibly have known, about love, a longing for love? It is hardly
oppressive, and yet a soft clarity emerges. Perhaps this is one of
Hardy's saving features, the way the poem so seldom feels a
burden on the reader, who can therefore slide into it and move
with it, sharing the experience. You might see what you think of
this. Meanwhile, there are many other poems in which, like this
one, an element of death or time past lets in the poet's sadness and

longing the more since the woman is beyond his reach. Again there is no need to read them all, but you might pick one or two now and read them without dwelling overlong on them. There is that somewhat alarming poem 'The Photograph' (p. 326), possibly 'sado-masochist' again (why is the poet 'compelled to heed'?), and its companions 'Thoughts of Phena' (p. 327) and 'The Torn Letter' (p. 150). In all three some physical non-human remains stand in for the loved woman herself. Then there is a group addressing girls Hardy had not seen for several decades. He writes on hearing of their deaths (Phena's too, as the subtitle of that poem tells us), or simply on looking back over his own long life. These poems include *Louie* (p. 316), 'To Louisa in the Lane' (p. 315), and 'To Lizbie Brown' (p. 313). Once more questions arise, of the poet's distance from these women he felt he loved, or longed to love. It seems, then, that he can't speak to some women, burns pictures and letters of others, fantasizes about yet more seen through windows or even (as in 'The Sunshade') never met at all, and recalls sadly yet more when it is too late. On our continuum the poet has come closer and closer to emotional involvement, but is not much closer to true encounter. Is this then something to do with the pattern of failed or frustrated love suggested earlier?

Let us now exemplify these observations by a longer look at a fairly substantial poem where the presence of the poet is intriguingly ambivalent. This is 'The Contretemps' (p. 148), I confess a favourite of my own although some critics see it as too much a *tour de force*. Please read it now, and then consider some of the many questions it raises. Our questions are a little more complex and detailed than usual.

1 The man and girl met, very nearly kissed, then each realized their mistake. Instead of leaving at once in embarrassment, the girl pours out her marital situation. Is that credible?
2 If that weren't enough, along come not only lover but husband as well. Almost at once too, for they saw the kiss or not-kiss themselves. What is more, 'Husband and lover then withdrew' – just like that (to the pub to share a consolatory jar, no doubt). Is that credible either?
3 The man and girl are left alone 'Forcing a parley what should do/We twain hearts caught in one catastrophe'. What catastrophe? Did the poet's girl-friend never appear? Why are they 'forced' to discuss anything at all?
4 Is the penultimate stanza, and lines three and four especially, the poem's message?
5 What of the poem's entire setting, the harbour bridge 'lamplit,

snowflaked, sloppiness around', and the hollow sound of the
channel ferry? What effect does it have? Is this what David
Wright meant in his introduction (page 21) about the nineteenth
century in Hardy's poetry: 'One sees it, smells it, hears it, feels
it'?

6 Does the poem feel autobiographical? Is the 'I' of stanza one
Thomas Hardy? Does the last stanza tell us?

DISCUSSION

You begin to notice sometimes, in Hardy's poetry, that you want
to call a poem unique, while equally feeling it to be so typical
that it couldn't possibly be by anyone but Hardy either. 'The
Contretemps' seems to me such a poem. I have tried not to load
these questions, but you may have caught the sense of where my
own feelings lie. I would simply suggest one reading. The poem is
fantasy, for the first stanza is something a young man might
dream of. If attractive girls do rush up and kiss you, it isn't often
they are complete strangers (if the girl in the poem was that), in
the romantic mist and snow of a November night, and on a
harbour bridge to boot. The girl is described in like manner to
that of 'A Countenance' and the setting is evocative too, but
neither husband nor lover get a detail. So the poet is selective, to
say the least. Equally the supposedly 'forced' parley is, perhaps,
forced by the circumstances, but it is the kind of force that draws
the participants in, if they indeed are to be envisaged as each
disappointed by the failure of another party to arrive.

Yet the setting is real enough for something 'biographical'
to have happened, not too far from fantasy, which might have
sparked the poem off. This would be speculation, although later
we shall see that the final stanza is like the last stanza of the last
poem of *Poems 1912–13*, and one or two other poems. The
description of the falling snow bears the imprint of not just experience but familiar, habitual experience. The suggestion, for me,
is that fantasy itself may be not far off realization at any time; that
life's chances may go in many directions, and that if 'naught
happens twice', as 'On the Departure Platform' has it, then that
itself means each new moment or incident is unpredictable. The
power of the poem lies in the interweaving of convincing detail
with a fantasy not too impossible, but not in the usual two-tiered
way of fantasy, such that solid everyday circumstance and impossible human encounter are thrown together. By its careful
phrasing, vivid without sensation, cumulative and successive yet
crucially omitting elements we might wonder about, and the

whole thrown in a casual rhythm economically sustained, a poise is maintained, putting the poem and its events just out of reach, yet still just believable.

Isn't that the hope and experience of most lovers? We begin to sense that Hardy's entire experience, or his observation of that of others, is of this just-out-of-reach consummation. The loved women are real – you might meet them anywhere, on bridges, in back rooms, on walks – yet they remain always just beyond you, not in being 'unattainable' in some romantic sense but because of some quite mundane block anyone would recognize. The poem does indeed feel like the nineteenth or early twentieth century, as Wright suggested, but perhaps because Hardy was trying to make readers feel they could have been there themselves. This aim makes for greater realism and, in a poet, yields up compulsively the detail which then goes vivid in words. There are one or two other poems in the same casually narrative mode as 'The Contretemps'. They are similarly loose-knit, the story falling easily into place with objects and clothing and bits of furniture or outdoor items picked up by the poem's relaxed rhythm. I'm thinking of 'The Harbour Bridge' (p. 175), 'Near Lanivet, 1872' (p. 343) and 'Honeymoon Time at an Inn' (p. 147), and will leave it to you here to try them if you wish to.

And so we come to *Poems 1912–13* (pp. 370–90), the group written within just a few months – some within weeks, perhaps days – of Emma Hardy's death on 27 November 1912. First, a bit of background information. William Morgan has shown that Hardy probably wrote more poems at this time than at any other time in his life.[2] Hardy himself made the selection of poems and arranged them in the order in which they are always printed. But they were not necessarily written in this order, as is shown by the dates at the bottom of some poems. Sometimes the month is given, sometimes just the year, sometimes nothing at all. Furthermore 'Rain on a Grave' (p. 373) is underwritten with '31 Jan., 1913' while 'The Voice' has 'December 1912', yet 'The Voice' is placed later in the sequence. In part then it seems the sequence's coherence is poetic rather than chronological, although a broad chronology does occur, as the opening poems make clear.

Because this is a group of connected poems we must approach them accordingly. Please first read the entire sequence. Do this fairly quickly, however, to get a sense of the main theme and pattern; but also because it is most important not to assume, *a priori*, that they are indeed Hardy's central body of work on love. They may be, but that is to be decided. We will then look at three of the poems more closely, but referring from time to time to the sequence's other poems. These three poems are 'The Going' (p. 370), 'The Voice' (p. 378) and 'The Phantom Horsewoman' (p. 385). Read these three more carefully, either all three together or as we come to each in our discussion.

Here first are some questions about the whole sequence, which you should now have read:

1 **What is the dominant mood? Is it elegy and mourning, or guilt and shock, or something else?**
2 **Remember our sight—sound distinction in Hardy's poems in the previous chapter. Who is speaking in each of the poems? Does the voice dominate the incident or setting in each case? How effective is the seaside setting?**
3 **What do you gather about Hardy's sense of the past? Why does he go back to recent past sometimes and to distant past elsewhere?**

Now re-read 'The Going' with special attention. Then apply the first three of our general questions to this poem. **Consider also how striking you think the poem is as an opener to the sequence. Is the language particularly awkward? Do you also notice a couple of references which we have already mentioned as actually occurring in Thomas's and Emma's real life?**

DISCUSSION

In light of all we have said so far, the opening poem is remarkable. It is full of questions, and to someone who is no longer there to answer.

> Why did you give no hint that night
> That quickly after the morrow's dawn
> And calmly, as if indifferent quite,
> You would close your term here, up and be gone
>   Where I could not follow
>   With wing of swallow
> To gain one glimpse of you ever anon!

He has spent his life straining for 'glimpses' of women of all kinds, through windows, across dance-halls and on foggy bridges. Yet now that the one always available to him for forty years is dead, he is lost. Some critics think the first line is defensive on Hardy's part, as though to insist he knew nothing of her ill-health. Yet the second stanza's opening is surely poignant, in the way it broken-heartedly tries to cope with the gap of silence – not a word, not a whisper of farewell – returned to more fully in the last three lines of stanza three. This third stanza is surely touchingly imaginative.

It is one of the two which is matched by what we know from outside the poem, and I quoted the relevant letter, to Florence Henniker, on page 22. The sudden picture we get in lines three and four, as of a family snapshot, enables us to feel as Hardy felt when he realized she would never be there in that familiar posture again. It differs thus from the more formal memory of stanza four, for that scene could never had been witnessed again, even if Emma had lived. This contrast between the recent and distant past, and Hardy's two moods in recalling them, comes over in snatchy fashion as of one plunged into grief in its very first moments. We feel what he felt.

The other reference is rather sad, and is in the first line of stanza five. You will remember that we said in Chapter 2 that often in their last period of shared life Thomas and Emma hardly spoke to each other. But Hardy doesn't recriminate; rather, he suggests more movingly that instead they could have revisited the places of their youth; and by this means he unites his recent and distant memories in a single act of recollection. The scene is set, by this poem, for us to experience the whole sequence as a total grief, facing many parts of the long shared life at once, taking each as personal mood and poetic form seem to direct, and enabling a catharsis for the stricken man to be reached.

The last lines are poignant in their fragmentary grammar and broken expression:

> . . . O you could not know
> That such swift fleeing
> No soul foreseeing
> Not even I – would undo me so!

Tom Paulin thought this last stanza was a rebuke,[3] as though Hardy felt Emma had died just to spite him. Maybe that's a little harsh, but certainly the sense of shock is more than elegaic. The abruptness of the shock is also the subject of the second and sixth poems of the sequence, 'Your Last Drive' (p. 371) and 'Without Ceremony' (p. 375); and the sequence then seems to reach some kind of first climax or deeper expression in one of Hardy's most famous poems – to many critics a main example of true greatness – 'The Voice'. This poem comes just before halfway through the sequence, and you should read it now. While doing so try to bear in mind the poems which have led up to it.

> Woman much missed, how you call to me, call to me,
> Saying that now you are not as you were
> When you have changed from the one who was all to me,
> But as at first, when our day was fair.

Can it be you that I hear? Let me view you, then,
Standing as when I drew near to the town
Where you would wait for me: yes, as I knew you then,
Even to the original air-blue gown!

Or is it only the breeze, in its listlessness?
Travelling across the wet mead to me here,
You being ever dissolved to wan wistlessness,
Heard no more again far or near?

    Thus I; faltering forward,
    Leaves around me falling,
Wind oozing thin through the thorn from norward,
    And the woman calling.

Consider this poem now in the light of the earlier poems and the
question of 'seeing' as discussed in the previous chapter. **Is the first
line of stanza two a key compound of sight and sound as we said
there? Is the final stanza such a compound? Do you notice any
difference between the writing in the first two stanzas and the last
two? And finally: is the poem one of Hardy's 'ghost' poems?**

DISCUSSION

This poem clearly contains the mix of sight and sound referred to
in Chapter 3. We observed there how some poems such as 'The
Darkling Thrush' (p. 218) switch from seeing to hearing when
eyesight seems inadequate to full understanding or knowledge.
Now, however, the distinction occurs much more humanly, in
a matter of loss and love. Suddenly, the pressing point is not
whether a woman is pretty, but that she is calling to him. The
poem seems to probe the voice all the time. Each stanza bar the
final short one begins with its pleading cry or question. Even when
he is compelled back to an image, the memorable 'air-blue gown',
that itself seems to drive him back to its oral cognate, the 'breeze'
in the next stanza which in the end presses strongest. (Why have
critics found 'air-blue' so right, do you think? It makes us think of
'sky-blue', but in more ethereal fashion; ghostly even, as though
Hardy is longing to believe in her nearby presence still.)

    There is also the strangely truncated last stanza. To see how
this works we must notice the overwhelming number of mono-
syllabic words in the first two stanzas, while in the last two the
longer words dominate: 'listlessness', 'travelling', 'dissolved',
'wistlessness' and then 'faltering' itself. I sense that Hardy sur-
rendered himself to the voice in the first two stanzas and let it play
over him. He then felt strong enough – or so the mood of the
poem suggests – to go on to some kind of explanation of what

was happening. But it comes to a sad stuttering halt, rather like
the close of 'The Going' did, and he finds he is not ready for that
after all. Grief must be more thoroughly purged. The stanza itself
'falters' – as so often in art, the thing said is the thing done – and
the elemental cold 'wind' and earlier 'wet mead' contrasts Emma's
ethereality, and weighs the poet down with the chillingly cold
world he is left with.

The sight–sound contrast shouldn't be laboured, but it does
begin to seem as though two distinct things are occurring across
the whole sequence. 'The Voice' underlines what has all along
been psychologically missing; a voice that speaks as well as a face
that radiates, in all the women he has aspired to, near or distantly.
(The woman narrator in 'A Trampwoman's Tragedy' was a conventional voice only.) Now, having raised Emma's voice into his
own consciousness – having at last *heard* her – Hardy begins to
add poems spoken from her side entirely. Please read either 'The
Haunter' (p. 377) or 'The Spell of the Rose' (p. 387) now for
comparison's sake, although I won't give them extended discussion here. Perhaps at last our continuum ends here: Hardy
discovers at last the woman's voice itself as one with his own. But
as well as this there is the visual aspect of *Poems 1912–13*. This
comes out in the many poems set in scenes on the cliffs and
beaches in Cornwall, where Hardy met and loved Emma when
they were young forty years before. This was touched on in stanza
four of 'The Going', and 'The Voice' at the end of stanza one. But
now, several poems of this kind enter the sequence. They include
'Beeny Cliff' (p. 382), 'At Castle Boterel' (p. 383), 'The Phantom
Horsewoman' (p. 385) and others. 'The Phantom Horsewoman',
as we shall see, is a particularly special example.

Will you please read 'The Phantom Horsewoman' again now?
It is also a famous poem. **Tom Paulin sees it as the climax of this
sequence.[4] Is that because these elements of sight and sound, so
important both, do now combine? Or is the visual picture of the
girl on horseback what really lasts? Who speaks the poem? All of
it? More broadly, consider too what the poet apparently comes to
learn about his life and himself from the whole experience the
poem conveys.**

DISCUSSION

For many readers the last stanza of 'The Phantom Horsewoman'
has become the prototype reference for Hardy's memory of the
young Emma when he brooded on her sudden death and his
ensuing loss. The picture of the 'ghost-girl-rider' who 'Draws rein

and sings to the swing of the tide' is very evocative. It reminds us perhaps of the late Victorian romantic heroines of middle-class story books. It obsessed Hardy himself it would seem, for the same picture is found in the other poems we have mentioned, including stanza four ('reining nigh me') of 'The Going' as we have seen, 'Beeny Cliff' and elsewhere. Yet this picture is not reached until the final stanza, even though we have learnt in stanza two that he sees 'as an instant thing,/More clear than to-day' this memory of the past, this 'phantom of his own figuring'. Does this mean then simply that this visualizing, so potent in Hardy always, is merely recalling the bit of the past that most matters?

Surely it means that. But the first stanza has already given another picture, that of Hardy himself. It is he that we see standing lonely on the sands at St Juliot, 'With moveless hands/ And face and gaze'. The 'gaze', a word you may recall we noticed in Chapter 3 (p. 35) in 'Nature's Questioning' (p. 288), is itself now being gazed at. Or, more accurately, he is gazing, but he himself is seen too, perhaps for what he is. But this is also what has made some critics wonder who is speaking in each stanza. The matter of the voice comes in as well. Some suggest that Emma is to be thought of as speaking throughout, others that she speaks at the start but that the poem's voice passes then imperceptibly into the inner broodings of Hardy himself. Others again feel that Hardy is speaking, standing off and looking back at himself. Whatever the truth, the seeing/being seen factor, considered as a feature of eyesight in Chapter 3, could here be thought of as culminating in a coming together, with eyesight seeing and object seen at last linked in true unity and clarity. I have to admit that, for myself, it is the visual scene that lingers, and the poet himself as now clearly part of it. In short, self-knowledge has been reached at last.

And the force of the poem, I suggest, lies in the fact of Hardy's loyalty to his vision, and so to his early love. For after conceding that the phantom is 'of his own figuring', he still doesn't shrink from evoking it, saving it in fact until the last stanza, the picture he wants us and himself to be left with. Hardy so often said in later years how wonderful those early times with Emma had been, and went on saying so long after their lustre had faded. He visited St Juliot in the spring of 1913, shortly after her death, and much regretted the trip. This fourth-stanza picture in 'The Phantom Horsewoman' is alluded to briefly, by implication, in the first stanza of 'The Voice', with Emma there heard calling that she is young again. As well as undeniably having an element

of desperation for the poet, this is surely too the shake-down of
memories in bereavement to the point of greatest tolerance, the
memory happiest and least painful to bear. Emma at last shares –
or so the poet would wish – in the poet's vision.

The phantom Emma rides emerging and disappearing against
the background of the Atlantic coast throughout *Poems 1912–13*.
It occurs equally often in the poems where she is herself speaking.
Hardy's dead wife, now loved when absent as she wasn't before,
is most seen when fully embodied as person, as autonomous self-
speaker to whom the poet can listen. It probably sounds senti-
mental to say so, but it might seem the epitome at last of married
love. In his novel *A Married Man* Piers Paul Read presents a
disloyal and indeed murderous wife who is then killed in an
accident. The husband, who knew of her disloyalty and crime, felt
that he was then married to her as he never had been in her life.
Whatever one may think of such suggestions, they evince again
what we see all along in Hardy and culminating here, the particular pattern of unfulfilled desire which has both drawn him on and
blocked him out in most of his sexual fantasies and youthful and
later flirtations or deeper friendships.

The psychoanalytic writer Jacques Lacan has had most influence in recent literary criticism on this matter of desire and its
poetic expression. Similar views were used by J. Hillis Miller in his
study of Hardy's work.[5] But Miller perhaps puts it differently. For
Miller, Hardy's characters fall in love at a distance. They are
fascinated by what they see, as we observed Hardy was in the
poem 'A Countenance'. But precisely because of the idealizing of
their desires into perfection – their belief that such desire could
never be satisfied – they stand off. In some cases this could be
because of the prosaic results when the love enters humdrum
reality of marriage and daily life, 'love unblinded'. For Miller the
lovers, and Hardy himself, realized they have been duped. Not by
the cunning deceptions of the female sex, but by their own unreal
expectations.

For Lacan, it is different. Here you might care to decide
which view you take, and how it enters the work of a poet. For
Lacan, desire itself is preferable, because desire itself is blissful in
its drawn-forward expectations, and its satisfaction must also be
its end.[6] Poetically this approach found its fullest expression in
John Keats's 'Ode on a Grecian Urn', where the figure of the lover
pursuing the maid, while fixed forever on the urn, is conceived
of as experiencing perpetual bliss. In psychoanalytical terms the
paired conception with desire is death. Sexual desire is based on
the fact that the urge to reproduce can never be satisfied alone; the

partner must be found, at which the organic species which is the human being has arrived at its only possible fulfilment. All this of course is envisaged as taking place at the psychobiological level: it is also a somewhat male viewpoint. Cultural factors or spiritual aspirations are not the point either – or, as Miller argued, are not the point until love is over, at which time the individual finds a gap left, filled by God in a traditional world.

More common in Hardy are poems about death, as of course in one sense are the *Poems 1912–13*. Indeed Hardy's obsession with death, which came home to him with such a shock when his own increasingly unnoticed companion was cut off so unexpectedly, is found all over his poetry, outside of the love poems as often as in them. It is to these we now turn in order to fill out further our account of Hardy's overall poetic psychology and its expression in so many poems. We must ask now whether the two things, love and death, are connected in his need for poetic expression. But once again, let's not beg the question at this point.

5. Death

The evidence that Hardy couldn't resist seeing death in life seems strong. He went to two public hangings when he was quite young, and for years after Emma's death took to making frequent excursions to Stinsford churchyard, often several in a week. Hardly surprisingly, the death in 1873 by suicide of perhaps his closest friend, Horace Moule, had the deepest effect on him. Hardy spent hours, in one sense years, in the company of the gloomier parts of the Bible and of ancient church architecture. In 1896 while on a trip to Europe he wrote to Florence Henniker, 'Why am I here again, & not underground!' The best-known quotation has other interpretations: 'For my part, if there is any way of getting a melancholy satisfaction out of life, it lies in dying, so to speak, before one is out of the flesh; by which I mean putting on the manners of ghosts, wandering in their haunts, and taking their views of surrounding things'.[1] Numerous poems, in part or whole, walk in the shadow of death and face its sadnesses.

The matter confronts us most sharply when we look at poems like 'Voices of Things Growing in a Churchyard' (p. 77), 'Friends Beyond' (p. 182) and 'Channel Firing' (p. 278). Now that you have built up some experience in reading Hardy's poetry I propose to do things a little differently in this chapter, and occasionally ask you to read two or three poems at once, instead of just one. Please now read these three poems.

1 What two features do the three poems have in common?
2 On their evidence, is the poet 'obsessed with death'?
3 Is the mood happy, morbid, restful or gruesome, would you say?
4 What part is played in the poems by material objects?

DISCUSSION

The two main shared features are clearly that all three poems are spoken in the voices of people dead and now buried, and that the voices come direct from their graves.

It is as though the poet is determined to put himself and us beyond the grave from the start. He isn't particularly mourning dear family or friends; rather he is seeing what things look like from their side. The first poem seems to be regular and without development. Each stanza portrays a different route by which the bodies in the graves decay and merge back into the vegetation around them. Fanny Hurd becomes flowers, Bachelor Bowring leaves on a wall, Thomas Voss yew, Lady Gertrude laurel, Eve Greensleeves pollen, and so on. The final stanza summarizes this; it attempts little addition. This is where one wonders whether the feeling is restful or morbid. Some readers might find the sense that real people have to end up like that, decomposing and rotting, very depressing indeed. But others I suppose would sense a tranquillity in that we are seen to rejoin an immediate natural and peaceful world by a simple and comprehensible process; and that, to me, is the main impression. Admittedly the refrain – 'All day cheerily,/All night eerily!' – might seem deliberately to leave both possibilities open, and indeed placing the eerie night second could also be taken to emphasize that aspect as the significant one. I can only reply that the movement is too even-paced to create scary disturbance, and that the transformations, the way in each stanza human body turns into natural growth, is a local and vivid rendering of a *philosophical* view of exact oneness and identity with the natural world. 'These flowers *are I*, poor Fanny Hurd', 'The Lady Gertrude ... *Am I* – this laurel that shades your head'.

In 'Channel Firing' the poet seems even more at home in his chosen setting, for the 'skeletons' awoken in their graves by gunfire at night sound like a group of rustics discoursing on political incompetence in the local pub – or at least, from their beds in the hospital. God (ward sister or bartender) lets them in on what all the noise is about, and the inmates grumpily complain about it and then go back to dominoes or sleep. On a higher-minded note one might compare the poem with Stanley Spencer's painting 'The Resurrection', although that painting too shows the risen bodies as coming from all walks of life. And in this poem the graveyard inhabitants are invoked as to their bodily decay even less than in 'Voices'. I don't know about you but I hardly notice the word 'skeleton' when I read this, it is so matter-of-fact. Far greater physical detail appears in the first two stanzas about the church itself at night, its rattling windows and the mice near the altar. Some of God's words in the poem suggest themes more permanent. It is of course a war poem – of sorts – as the date indicates, but references suggesting length of time (for example the antiquated phrase 'for Christes sake') underline the main theme of God's judgement after death, on human action over the centuries. Yet this judgement is hardly menacing or cruel, and the dead's tranquillity is not much disturbed.

The third poem, 'Friends Beyond', was probably written first of these three, which may indicate why the speaker is an ordinary person still alive – indeed Hardy himself presumably – and the voices are still left explicitly as his imagination at work. This poem is the best-known of these three and indeed is one of Hardy's most famous. And at first reading at least it certainly seems to have more in it than the other two. The first few lines are reminiscent, though in contrast, of Gray's 'Elegy Written in a Country Churchyard', a poem Hardy esteemed highly. The clear difference is that while Gray insists that his buried villagers are unknowns, here a list of names is rolled confidently out at the start. That is not to make them famous after all, and their equality despite class rank seems to be emphasized; it certainly is later. As with Gray too, the scene is twilight; the 'mothy curfew-tide'; and the remarkably apt comparison of these murmuring voices to 'stillicide', the drip-drip of water from a cave's roof.

But there the comparison with Gray ends. By contrast, we note the terms of the very first thing the dead say: 'triumph', 'achievement', 'success'. The voices speak quietly, but with firm confidence. If this poem can indeed be dated in the mid-1890s, as many critics think, then Hardy was writing at the end of a period of great national industrial prosperity. The result may be read two ways. Either Hardy is soberly using the competitive language of the day, or it is ironic. If 'death gave all that we possess', this could mean either that death gave them all they now have in death, or that it gave *away* what is now superfluous, namely, all the possessions hard-won in the new materialism. But whichever way one takes it, this duality seems to underline the matter of worldly success as past.

In stanza six the speakers then separate to yield up, willingly and even with relief, their worldly goods, concerns and problems. They rejoin in stanza nine to state they are not interested any more in news and gossip, scandal or glory, town or country. And since this long section ends only six lines before the poem's close, it may well contain the poem's main purport; it certainly feels so to me. And what is noticeable surely is that every kind of worldly activity is covered, including the perfectly laudable and reasonable. The first possession yielded is not Lady Susan's jewels or secret letters but William Dewy's 'old bass-viol', and the second is that bastion of Victorian life, the family, which the squire lets go as though it were nothing. Is there any suggestion he was unhappy with it in life, or is death's calm shown to be coming as a surprising revelation of far greater joys? All these things are 'haps', Hardy's common word for all life's combinations and outcomes, but they are also its 'crosses'. The poem's central pressure comes surely from the relentless if quiet insistence on naming *all* the things which the dead can now relinquish with equanimity. It is as though to show that, whatever they name, they are still composed; there are still no regrets.

To throw more light on this matter generally, let's now look at the conventional poem which looks sadly at death: the elegy. One so drawn to our mortality as Hardy was might be expected to have written such poems, and indeed he did. Examples include 'After the Last Breath' (p. 70), 'Molly Gone' (p. 73) and 'Paying Calls' (p. 75). Please read these three poems now. Then answer for yourself the following questions. Your answer to the first question may show you a link between the other three which are each on a separate poem.

1 What is the main difference between these three poems and the first three we looked at in this chapter?
2 How does the content of 'After the Last Breath' compare with that of 'Friends Beyond'?

3 What does all the descriptive detail in 'Molly Gone' achieve?
4 If this chapter hadn't explicitly raised it, would you have
known 'Paying Calls' was about death?

DISCUSSION

The clear difference, surely, is that whereas voices spoke from the
graves themselves in the first three poems, in these last three it is
the survivor of the dead who speaks.

According to the usual definitions, elegy is that genre in
which a survivor addresses a dead loved person, or admired or
respected people (e.g. dead national figure, or victims of a disaster),
or else reflects on them, in such a way as to end up finding
consolation in a more general philosophical attitude. In a well-
known article[2] Robert Circasa suggested this could be seen as a
turning away from the dead, leaving them safely buried and our
grief allayed. This left them at rest and ourselves calmed too, so
that we could turn back with new steadiness to our own lives.
Circasa felt that Hardy had not done this – perhaps not tried to –
in the *Poems 1912–13*, for he had remained with the dead
companion to the end; and my suggestion now is that Hardy did
not do this either in the poems we have seen so far. Even in
'Friends Beyond', where the dead seem to have found deep peace
in their graves, we do not leave them behind. In the poem's very
last phrase they still 'murmur mildly to me now'. And so what
apparently matters to the poet is that he is working out and
voicing a conscious philosophy of how the state of death is to be
thought of. The question is whether our latest trio which you have
just read are different. I think they are.

Take 'After the Last Breath'. Surely the whole tenor, and
especially the list in the first two lines of what no longer matters,
is similar in a broad way to the things that no longer matter to the
dead speakers in 'Friends Beyond'. And the list of now-superfluous
bedroom and medical necessities has a similar tendency. There is
even the word 'achievement' at the end, as in the other poem,
though this time it is 'Wrongers' who are defeated. But the difference is that it is the survivor who speaks. Certainly it is unusual
as elegy goes, for it seems very immediate. As the title seems to
suggest, she has only just died, perhaps moments before. We only
see 'by littles' what the general principle of elegy is likely to be. It
is as though not the whole life – and it is Hardy's own mother
after all who has died – but the strain up to the parting, is what is
removed. But even so, although we don't come to full elegy, we
prepare for it.

In 'Molly Gone', on the other hand, there is indeed a recalling of the life. The death itself is not mentioned. But Molly herself is hardly mentioned; rather, each stanza seems to aim at celebrating the seasons and natural settings which the poet remembers as what he and Molly shared; summer, planting, jauntings, singing. And the refrain 'no more' at the start of each stanza is itself a 'turning-away', perhaps, by the poet, from the shared past he must now put behind him. Molly was Mary Hardy, the poet's sister; he was devoted to her but this was not one of his *amours*. The poet's ending seems to be happiness, then, to place her back in that wider nature by a kind of pantheistic affirmation, and the sense that in concert with nature life goes on afterwards and is what survives. It is almost as though, since he and Molly had already wrapped themselves joyfully into the natural world, death made little difference. Death itself is deflected away, and made therefore to seem to enable a new phase of life without the dead one who is mourned.

The point is made further by comparison with the third poem, 'Paying Calls'. Here the poet seems to want to emphasize friendship. The word 'friends' appears in the first two of the four stanzas, and 'at home' in the third. The point is opposite from that of 'Molly Gone', where celebration of past sharing out in the natural world was evoked. Here the emphasis that this can't continue is made by the very absence of the detail that saturated 'Molly Gone'. The friends all stay 'at home'. But they 'spoke not to me' as the last line tells, and only then do we suddenly gather the import of the word 'mound' earlier in the stanza. The gentle sad song-like mood ('Strayed here a mile and there a mile') tells, however, of a poem known by its poet before it began; that is to say, the death-sadness has already been put away in immediate terms. And so we are left with a general very brief reflection. The dead are 'at home' by being dead, and all is well: yet equally as they 'spoke not' to the poet they too have been in effect settled into the past, and life for the survivor, however sadly without them, continues.

It might be rash to generalize from this small sample. Yet the elegiac letting-go, in one way or another, seems to be present. In two cases, furthermore, these are poems on members of Hardy's own family, in the third case people buried in his own local-churchyard. The poetic compulsion to write of death – the tendency to fill its void with words when the listener has gone, and so subdue harsh grief by making it soft melancholy – is met in the ordinary elegiac way. All the more then must we look elsewhere for explanation about Hardy's wider, more unusual death-poems.

For these few elegies, carrying the distinctive Hardy note and
voice as they certainly do, tell us nothing further about his transformation into poetry of other, wider, perhaps eccentric or idiosyncratic death-attitudes.

For Hardy wrote several poems about death where not only
no one has died but where the poet sees himself as in the death-
wish situation. He reflects on death simply for what it means to
himself or presses on himself. The poem 'Wessex Heights' (p. 293)
and the three 'In Tenebris' poems (pp. 290–2) have often been so
taken. All four poems were almost certainly written very soon
after Hardy decided to switch from novels to poetry in about
1896 or so. They may even themselves have been a help in leading
up to that decision. If they were, they suggest an attitude hardly
promising, if a positive approach to a new career was wanted. Of
course, one must allow for Hardy's desperately low spirits after
the response to the publication of 'Jude the Obscure'.

It would take much space to comment on all four poems and
in any event I don't want this chapter to be solely a list of
commentary notes on various poems. Please now read the 'In
Tenebris' poems if you choose, but certainly 'Wessex Heights'
which I will then discuss. Having read 'Wessex Heights' consider
the following questions before going on to the discussion.

1 Are the ghosts in the poem real (to Hardy) or just metaphors?
2 How literally does he feel the last line of the first stanza?
3 Why does Hardy use such long lines in this poem, and with
   what effect?

DISCUSSION

In 'Wessex Heights' the poet stands on a hill somewhere in
Wessex. Up there, he says, 'I seem where I was before my birth,
and after death may be.' He rehearses most painfully what it is 'in
the lowlands' that rejects him. He has no comrade, people are
'dubious and askance' and, as a result, he is 'tracked by phantoms'.
These phantoms recur throughout the poem. They hardly seem
ghost-story ghosts, yet they are real enough to the poet. His
lengthy, dragging line, which feels too long for itself, as though
every particle of oppressive thought must be exorcised, goes
oppressively through all the woes. It searches each one by one as
though to see if an exhaustive expression of them can poetically
yield up their real furtive natures.

The last four stanzas, especially the three leading up to the
very last, seem very compelling. Compelling, that is, as a real

expression of something within the poet, not now self-indulgence, which he sees as 'ghostly'. In the first of these stanzas he can't go down into Salisbury or on to its plain. In the next he sees ghosts. In the third he feels, in bitter and compelling accuracy, how little he means to, presumably, Florence Henniker, although you don't have to assume it is her. My own sense too is that the contents of the sandwich, those 'ghosts' he names, are or were real people he may not be actually seeing as ghosts now up on the heights, but whose vivid and pressing memory-presence make him think soberly of what ghosts might be. Hardy probably wondered whether such memories don't in some way actually merge into true ghost-presence for certain sensitive people. The question then is of how that connects with his wider feelings in general about death. In stanza four Hardy distances himself from himself, steps out of his own body to look back at himself: ' . . . my simple self that was,/And is not now, and I see him watching, wondering what crass cause/Can have merged him into such a strange continuator as this'. It does seem as though the attitude that projected these lines is the same one that enabled the projection of himself into the dead speakers in the first three poems we looked at. It seems that Hardy doesn't only sense he would truly find relief in such a position, in being dead-in-life. He also senses that, as a result, his whole poetic voice here is a voice from the dead. That is, he seems to see poetry itself as that strange language which isn't social interaction, but is a self-contained object of language which the reader can take or leave.

I suggest these notions as a way in to those other poems where ghosts seem to be evoked explicitly. A long and rather obscure one is 'In Front of the Landscape' (p. 80), which has an excellent commentary by J. Hillis Miller.[3] But let's move now to a more easily graspable poem, and here I introduce the one poem this book will deal with – or even mention – which is not in our text, David Wright's selection. The poem is short and is called 'The Garden Seat'. Here it is in full:

Its former green is blue and thin,
And its once firm legs sink in and in;
Soon it will break down unaware,
Soon it will break down unaware.

At night when reddest flowers are black
Those who once sat thereon come back;
Quite a row of them sitting there,
Quite a row of them sitting there.

With them the seat does not break down,
Nor winter freeze them, nor floods drown,

For they are as light as upper air,
They are as light as upper air!

Here are just two questions about it.

1 Does Hardy *actually believe* in the existence of the ghosts
  depicted here?
2 He achieves the poem's effect by some remarkable poetic techniques. What are they?

DISCUSSION

This is surely a very eerie poem. I have to say I find it very
haunting. But the question this poem confronts us with is very
simple. It is that of how much Hardy really did see these ghosts,
or at least really believe they were there, and how much that itself
is connected with what he then writes about them as a poet. Indeed
the two questions I asked above could be combined into a single
one in literary-critical terms. Does Hardy's skill as a poet invoke
ghostliness here, or do real ghosts, or something imagined to be
that, bring forth such poetry?

Hardy said once that he would give ten years of his life to see
a real apparition, 'an authentic, indubitable spectre'. There is
record of one occasion when he did, or at least so reported it, at
the door of Stinsford church. Hardy had just placed a sprig of
holly on the grave of his grandfather. The ghost appeared, Hardy
answered, and the ghost entered the church. Hardy followed, but
there was no one there. This incident and Hardy's wishes are well
reported in Dennis Taylor's book,[4] where indeed his whole third
chapter 'Hardy's Apocalypse' is an excellent parallel commentary
to our own topic here of Hardy on death. In this poem 'The
Garden Seat' the aim does seem that of leaving no doubt about
what he is evoking. By contrast the 'voices' in the first three poems
looked at in the present chapter were a contrivance. Hardy catches
in them a real or imagined after-life possibility, but surely we
weren't led to believe he actually heard, or thought he heard, the
voices of Lady Susan, William Dewy, Fanny Hurd and the rest.
But in 'The Garden Seat' the opening emphasis on the fact that the
seat's legs push into the soft turf when someone sits on them, can't
be escaped as to its implication. It is a straightforward fact about
garden seats (ours is always sinking in this fashion). Since the
poem implies nothing but the opposite inference for the night-
time, there seems little doubt as to what he is talking about.

The effect is enhanced perhaps by the chilling symbolic significance of 'red' and 'black' in stanza two; the startling exclama-

tion mark at the end: but mainly by the dreamlike, atemporal sound achieved by repeating the last line of what are already short stanzas. There is, furthermore, the continuous single rhyme throughout those refrains. Do you notice something, too, about the earlier rhymes in each case, thin/in, black/back, drown/down? The second rhyme has the same starting consonant as the first, bar the opening pair where it ('in') has none at all. Most rhyming pairs in poetry have an identical main syllable with a different opening consonant; house/mouse, fearful/tearful, and so on. Here, by contrast, the sameness of consonant supports the run-through quality of the rhyme, making for a hollow continuous undernote to the whole poem, as though accompanying something from a timeless world.

But this monorhyme technique is found in other ghost poems of Hardy's too. In 'Who's in the Next Room?' (p. 303), which we considered in Chapter 3 (pp. 32–3), you may have noticed that the 'who?' rhyme goes right through each stanza, countering a single alternate rhyme in each. In 'The Ghost of the Past' (p. 61) the strange jaunty effect comes along with the repetition of the second half of line one to make line two. This isn't exclusive to the ghost poems, and you will recall we found it in 'A Trampwoman's Tragedy' (p. 115). But it is backed up in 'The Ghost of the Past' further by the repetition of words (instead of having rhymes for them) at line-endings later in each stanza. The words themselves are compelling, weighted: housekeeping/housekeeping/, companionship/companionship, troths/troths, embrowned/embrowned, skeleton/skeleton. This repetition seems similar to the repetition of the first two lines as again the last two in each stanza of a poem we looked at in Chapter 1, 'Overlooking the River Stour' (p. 346). It turned out there, if you remember, that all the while the poet had had something else nagging at his mind, a fact – though not the thing itself – referred to in the final stanza. It's as though these repetitions mean the poet is somehow sealed in to something which he is drawn repeatedly to invoke. The title here, 'The Ghost of the Past', might reveal it. Ghosts, death poems, elegies, are usually evocations of the past. Indeed, this theme of the evocation of the past turns out to be widespread in Hardy. So what can we say about it?

We have seen that while Hardy does write conventional (which doesn't mean insincere) elegies too, he also has strange and perhaps idiosyncratic poetic approaches to death. Voices speak from the grave, ghosts are evoked and even felt in their presence, dancers turn into skeletons, and (in poems like 'Shelley's Skylark') small creatures decompose and change the earth where that happens. Death is more indirectly, but clearly, visualized in, for example, 'Near Lanivet, 1872' (p. 343), where the woman leaning wearily against a riding post suddenly looks like a crucifixion scene. People die off one by one, as in 'The Five Students' (p. 418). In 'At the Draper's' (p. 123) and 'Seen by the Waits' (p. 95) they are in someone's way by continuing to live. In 'Life and Death at Sunrise' (p. 57), as the Bishop of Salisbury reminded us for his own case, the day someone is born is the day someone else dies. But all these poems, I suggest, in some way show how Hardy emphasizes the past, time passing itself. Sometimes it is more explicit. 'Molly Gone' evoked past scenes strongly. Rather differently 'Aquae Sulis' (p. 233), with its 'filmy shape unsepulchred' is a ghost poem of historical import.

Let us recall that, in writing of love, Hardy was suddenly compelled in later years to write poems about women he had loved when young many years before. In Chapter 4 (p. 43) we briefly cited 'To Lizbie Brown' (p. 313), 'Louie' (p. 316) and others. The same was true of 'Molly Gone' in the present chapter, this time a blood relative. In a poem called 'The Paphian Ball' (p. 188) we are told at the end not only that the story is past but that the narrator we have been hearing is also long dead. At the end of 'The Contretemps' (p. 148), it seemed, of the four in the story only one now survives. At the end of 'Where the Picnic was' (p. 389) from *Poems 1912–13* one is dead, two more have departed the scene. Many years have gone by, too, between the events of 'Reminiscences of a Dancing Man' (p. 97) and its telling by the poet. William Morgan[5] dates this poem at 1895, and yet the events in it are clearly from Hardy's time in London in the 1860s.

Another very important poem with this emphasis on the past is 'During Wind and Rain' (p. 419). I won't ask you formal questions about this poem or give it extended discussion but I do most strongly recommend you to read this one, of the several I am briefly naming in these few pages. In 'During Wind and Rain' there are two time-sets. The young people's happiness set in the house and garden in the long distant past are contrasted, in each stanza's final line, by an evocation of the decayed present. Indeed the contrast between past and present here is given greater richness and poignancy by the parallel contrast between remembered youthful achievement in a life worth having, and the fragility that, as with any life, it turns out to have by the end. Tom Paulin, Dennis Taylor, Donald Davie and Harold Bloom are among those who have seen this short piece as one of Hardy's finest poems. Bloom calls it 'as good a poem as our century has given us'.[6] Is this poem's high rating connected to its evocation of a past long dead, do you think, and the connection of that with individual death? What do you make of the adjectives so carefully placed in the last line of each stanza?

The question broadly then is that of how Hardy's many evocations of death relate to his obsessive memory of the past more generally. My suggestion is, that memory of the past is close to Hardy's approaches to evoke death itself by some way *other* than the usual elegiac. At one level that is simple and understandable. Hardy's poetic career, as we know, took place in his later years, from his mid-fifties until death in his eighties. He would frequently have looked back across a long life. He sensed whole decades of past time at once; and he once said, in an often-quoted statement, that he could bury an incident or emotion in his mind and disinter it decades later – on occasion, as much as forty years.[7] But it is more than this. Perhaps you gathered from the *Poems 1912–13* the feeling of desperation as well as elegy; the need to ask Emma why she went so quickly, to hear her voice again, even to invent it as a ghost itself. Accompanying this was his own revisiting of the spot in Cornwall by the sea where he first met her, also forty years back, and which provided the setting of so many of the 1912–13 poems. Only then was he freed to write the more formal elegy, 'Where the Picnic was', with which the sequence ends. If only, he seems to say, he had noticed her more during her life.

But don't so many of Hardy's poems have this 'if only' feeling? Didn't many we have considered already, like 'A Thunderstorm in Town' (p. 358) and 'On the Esplanade' (p. 323) and 'Overlooking the River Stour' and 'A Trampwoman's Tragedy' and 'At Lulworth Cove a Century Back' (p. 214)? But the 'if only' feeling is not a present wistful fantasy, such as, if only I had a million dollars. It is always *afterwards*; it occurs in the context of a dimension of time passing over which humans have little control. Hillis Miller and Dennis Taylor refer to it not as 'if only' so much as 'too late'.[8] A Hardy poem, it seems, discovers knowledge; it learns, but 'too late', and the poems end again and again with some new insight coming out of the very failure or human mortality or other limitation which enabled that knowledge at all. And this, perhaps, gives us an insight into Hardy's attitude to death and his perspective on it.

It is a complex matter and we will return to it in the final chapters. Hardy's novels are permeated with this same feeling of arrival on the scene too late, when the time for effective action is past, or when a new factor has changed the situation. *The Mayor of Casterbridge* is probably the chief example, while *Tess* and *Jude* are also permeated with it. It seems then that this feeling of belated action is not peculiar to the poems; rather, the poems reveal the deep personal thrust in Hardy as to the emotive and indeed universal significance of such things.

More generally as to the poetry: we said near the start of this chapter that the dead who speak seemed to know more; also that in death they found relief. We will look at the psychoanalytic technicalities about the 'death-wish' in a later chapter. But we might now ask, then, whether this wish is a longing to end the sequence of events in which one always finds out, too late to change it, what one should have done or should have known. Death, paradoxically, is the final too-late condition; there is no further any opportunity to alter anything at all; yet for the very same reason its totality is a release from the repetition of any such circumstance ever again. Poetically, this consideration might seem to tie in with the wish to end the endless spate of deferrals of desire mentioned when we were talking in the last chapter about indirect love. We might also ask whether the closure or non-closure of Hardy's poems is what causes the quick switch on to yet another poem, resulting in the thousand or so in the collected poems, as Hillis Miller points out.[9] You might care to mentally arrange in your own mind the poems you have read, on a continuum from those which seem to have a solidity, a settlement of their own (perhaps 'Under the Waterfall', p. 339, and 'Life and Death at Sunrise') through to those which seem simply to push one on to the next temporary alighting place – perhaps 'The Sunshade', p. 138, and 'A Thunderstorm in Town'. And here, too, is the point to say that I hope by now you are in the habit of reading at least some of the poems we can only mention in passing, and perhaps finding further examples of your own. You will certainly find it rewarding to do so.

We shall also ask, in our final chapters, how this feeling of mortal inadequacy, this too-lateness, is found more generally in Hardy's time, and how much the widespread feeling of a century's completion ('*fin-de-siecle*') was taken up by the sensitivities of an ageing poet of that age. You may recall the phrase 'The Century's corpse outleant', and its import, in 'The Darkling Thrush' (p. 218). Consider, for example, at least the titles of 'God's Funeral', 'At Madame Tussaud's in Victorian Years' and others. They might lead you to wonder about this wider question and setting. However, before proceeding to our concluding chapters, we should first look at the contentious question of Hardy's poetic language. This can't, of course, just be separated from the poems' general subject matter and import, but in looking at the language we can endeavour to bear that connection in mind.

6. Language

We have now referred, at least in passing, to several dozen poems. I hope you think the method is working, and that you have felt free either to keep to fewer poems thoroughly or to range further and wider from the start. However, all readers will doubtless be relieved to know that this present chapter will confine itself entirely to poems which have already been at least mentioned, however cursorily.

You may have realized by now that Hardy's poetry is regarded, by admirers and detractors alike, as somewhat eccentric and quirky. It apparently makes rules for itself about not only poetry but grammar and language too, and introduces weird kinds of vocabulary. We probably find this all easier to take today than critics did when it first appeared. We are now long used to neologisms and strange and striking devices in advertising, media, ethnically different uses of English, and more and more incursions from other languages as education and travel increase. Even so, Hardy's uniqueness – as I take it to be – remains, and our new understandings may even make it easier to see in his work the creative use of language his supporters claim for it. So it is still worth a special look at this language itself, and that is the purpose of this chapter.

What have you most noticed? Words, phrases, unexpected forms? New metaphorical angles like a moorhen 'Planing up shavings of crystal spray' in 'Overlooking the River Stour' (p. 346)? Seemingly invented words like 'wistlessness' in 'The Voice' (p. 378)? Awkwardnesses surprisingly successful or rather more ham-fisted? I'm going to plunge straight in with a frankly mechanical list of some of what I have found; but I hope before reading this you will list some of your own discoveries. My list is a little hand-to-mouth, not seeking a systematic structure, and that is maybe fittingly like Hardy's approach to poetry itself. Later on we will suggest a few resulting principles, but not yet.

1 Strange words. *unhope, deedily, liefer, scath, enray, out-leant, continuator, enarch, unlipped, slayless, wistlessness, lours, unblinded, inurns, grinterns, interlune, parle, webby, quoin, whangs, nimb, vulturine, chasmal.* One could add many more to this list. Some of these words were still current in Hardy's time, but many are old words he resuscitated, and many more are his own coinages. An excellent guide to all these uses is Ralph W. V. Elliott's work (see Bibliography). In underlining the importance of the Oxford English Dictionary's compilation in the later part of the nineteenth century, Dennis Taylor suggests that '(Hardy) is most faithfully the poet of the OED'.[1]

2 Hyphenated words of Hardy's own invention. *summer-seeming, ail-stricken, Earth-secrets, rain-reek, foam-fingered, air-blue, stream-shine, drop-drenched, passionate-eyed, paddock-path, foot-folk, bereavement-pain, spirit-guise, mellow-faced, dust-paven, scoop-eyed, pharos-shine, mist-imbued, life-fraught, time-lines* and countless others. Some of these are two words that might ordinarily have come together anyway. Many pairings were used by Hardy once only.

3 Ordinary words but used for normally unacceptable grammatical function. A common one is 'obscure' as a noun, as in 'murked obscure' in 'Near Lanivet, 1872' (discussed later in this chapter) and 'A man shows in the obscure' in 'A Hurried Meeting' (p. 176). Consider also 'of gentle and rough' (i.e. gentle and rough people) in 'On the Departure Platform' (p. 364), 'the waters' medicinal pour' at the end of 'Aquae Sulis' (p. 233), 'shines' as noun in 'On the Esplanade' (p. 323) and 'wile' in 'To Lizbie Brown' (p. 313) You may find many more cases.

4 Hardy likes to play tricks with language in a more diffused way. Here are two examples:

(a) 'Voices of Things Growing in a Churchyard' (p. 77) has a second short line which is repeated in every stanza as refrain. It is ' "Sir or Madam!" ' and is addressed by each dead person to the graveyard visitor in turn. But in the final stanza that narrator uses it impersonally himself: '– And so these maskers breathe to each/Sir or Madam . . .'. A small ironic counterpoint is achieved; and such techniques enable some small emphasis change, or a new small insight, in each case. There is a parallel example in 'Fetching Her' (p. 350).

(b) Concealed wordplay. We saw one case in 'The Sunshade'

(p. 138). The poet describes the skeleton parasol he has found on the beach. The first stanza ends:

> Merely a naked sheaf of wires! —
> Twenty years have gone with their livers and diers
> Since it was silked in its white or pink.

A clear pun on 'livers' (as anatomy), but not until a few lines later do we come to the phrase 'the hue of its dyes' and see that 'diers' was a pun too, reaching forward to 'white and pink' at the first stanza's end. Hardy seems drawn especially to this wordplay when talking of colours. In 'A Light Snow-Fall after Frost' (p. 168) there was a reference to colour too, as you may remember from Chapter 1. The man with the ruddy beard and green coat, by virtue of those features, 'Wears something of the dye/Of the berried holm-trees that he passes nigh.' Can we believe Hardy didn't at least notice the die/buried echo there?

5 Verse forms. This is an enormous subject, and I can best refer you at once to Dennis Taylor's most recent book on it (see the Bibliography). Hardy ransacked ancient ballads, popular music-hall songs and Victorian hymns for forms to copy or adapt. He used hundreds of verse-forms, in fact virtually never repeated one exactly, and invented a large number himself. Here are just two examples of his borrowings, both changing their originals:

(a) this is the first stanza of 'The Dutchess' [*sic*] of Monmouth's Lamentation for the Loss of Her Duke',[2] a broadside ballad of the seventeenth century:

> 'Loyal hearts of *London City*, Come I pray, and sing my Ditty,
>   Of my Love that's from me gone;
> I am slighted and much spighted, and am left alone to mourn.'

Compare that with the stanza of 'Friends Beyond' (p. 182).

(b) a well-known Victorian hymn begins:

> Christ, whose glory fills the skies,
> Christ, the true, the only light,
> Sun of righteousness, arise,
> Triumph o'er the shades of night;
> Dayspring from on high be near,
> Daystar, in my heart appear.

A similar rhyme form is found in other hymns, 'Rejoice, the Lord is King', 'O quickly come, dread judge of all', 'Christ in highest heav'n enthron'd' and more. The line-length varies a little from hymn to hymn, as it does in Hardy's poem 'The

Dream is – Which?' (p. 394) which I suggest as a comparison.
Hardy's stanza also has six lines. But the rhyme scheme – a-b-
a-b-c-c – is exactly reversed. Hardy goes a-a-b-c-b-c. This is a
typical modification on his part, and in this poem, which you
may recall we mentioned when talking of the 'ghost' poems,
the result is a curious eerie feeling of falling-away in each
stanza. The matching couplet which ought to be each stanza's
climax comes at the start, and so leads to a tailing-off.
(Also here, as in 'The Garden Seat' and other ghost-poems,
Hardy keeps a monorhyme going. It underlines the haunting
atmosphere.)

6 Hardy frequently capitalizes abstractions. 'Bygone',
'Present' and 'Past' in 'The Ghost of the Past' (p. 61), 'Beloved'
in 'Something Tapped' (p. 398), 'their Shining Land' in 'The
Impercipient' (p. 228), and several instances in 'Nature's Questioning' (p. 288) where 'an Automaton', 'some Vast Imbecility',
'some high Plan' and 'We the Forlorn Hope over which Achievement strides', equally all refer to other-world entities, or our own
seen from that perspective. You might wonder how far these are
religion-substitutes in a newly scientific age, or an irony about any
such possibility.

7 More widely again, Hardy frequently packs two or three
heavy unexpected adjectives and nouns together in resilient-
sounding conjunctions. 'An eyelid's soundless blink' in 'Afterwards' (p. 304), 'the delicate bosom's defenceless round' in 'The
Photograph' (p. 326), 'in Time's stayless stealthy swing,/Uncom-
promising rude reality' from 'God's Funeral' (p. 230), 'blast-
beruffled plume' from 'The Darkling Thrush' (p. 218), 'Such
magic-minted conjurings' in 'Fetching Her'. Since in the same
poems he can write lines like 'then I vented a cry of hurt, and
averted my eyes' and 'he was a man who used to notice such
things', you might ask why he also deliberately included such
verbal ballast.

8 As will be seen below, I think this feature ties to a more
diffuse, and very frequent, use of the same thing. The poetry
is spattered with phrases like 'mothy and warm' ('Afterwards'),
'packs of years' ('The Photograph'), 'In a careworn craze' ('The
Phantom Horsewoman', p. 385), 'mental scenes no longer orbed/
By love's young rays' from 'Beyond the Last Lamp' (p. 167), 'the
embers in hearthside ease' ('The Oxen', p. 229), 'The lamplit,
snowflaked, sloppiness around' from 'The Contretemps' (p. 148).
Don't they all feel rather unflowing, selected, choice? These again
appear alongside such simplicities as 'And there alone still stood

we two', or the economical rendering of a speech in one sentence; ' "Little, I knew,/Madam, you had a third!" ', (both from 'The Contretemps').

9 All this brings us finally to Hardy's curious grammar and semantics; his supposed 'mistakes' although many of them aren't that even despite their oddity. Sometimes it is simply economy pared down to the near-unacceptable, as in 'The Going' (p. 370): 'Where I could not follow/With wing of swallow'. The second line would normally be something like 'as with the wing of a swallow'. There are dozens – hundreds – of such small curiosities. 'Must own me foiled!' 'The Abbey-Mason' (p. 130) for 'must own I am foiled'; 'There plays and sings/A lady unseen a melody undefined' ('On the Esplanade'); 'Somebody muttering firm in a language new' (i.e. 'somebody mutteringly firmly in a new language) in 'Who's in the Next Room?' (p. 303); 'I kept my seat in my search for a plea' in 'Faintheart in a Railway Train' (p. 317); 'in vain do I urge my unsight/To conceive my lost prize' ('Thoughts of Phena', p. 327); 'Over the mirrors meant/To glass the opulent' ('The Convergence of the Twain') (p. 277); and enough more to keep us going for the rest of this book and longer.

10 Yet the same poet, in Paulin's terms so spiky and fricative,[3] can write a poem like 'Paying Calls' (p. 75) as well; and for blank absence itself just say ('Thoughts of Phena') 'Not a line of her writing have I,/Not a thread of her hair'. He writes whole stanzas like this one ('Wessex Heights' p. 293):

> As for one rare fair woman, I am now but a thought of hers,
> I enter her mind and another thought succeeds me that she prefers;
> Yet my love for her in its fulness she herself even did not know;
> Well, time cures hearts of tenderness, and now I can let her go.

So what do we make of this weird inventory? Gathering examples like this helps to bring out features that are numerous but otherwise dispersed; but equally by taking them all out of context it may drain their effect. At this point we might broadly identify a kind of rich anarchy in Hardy's approach, a determination to shape *all* aspects of poetry and language in his own way. As Samuel Hynes has pointed out, English poets at the end of the nineteenth century felt the language was exhausted;[4] Hardy's poetry has traces of a lost order. We know various things; for example, that Hardy bought dictionaries and grammars when young and used them for years, and that he collected song metres. Surely most interesting of all, he is on record as having often written 'poems' made of nonsense syllables first, and then 'filled' them with whatever content he had decided upon.

The reason for these strange usages, I suggest, is paradoxical. Hardy rates economy and lucidity so high as priorities that to get them he will infringe our ordinary expectations of language. That is paradoxical, of course, because if we are bewildered by the seeming oddities and errors, there may be no lucidity after all. And indeed that is what happened, with many early critics dismissing him as a novelist who had unwisely decided on a fresh start late in life. Other critics (for example Lytton Strachey) began to see the point, and after a while came the curious event of critics noticing that Hardy was good when really he ought to be bad. T. S. Eliot once said Hardy often attains the sublime without first passing through the stage of being good. Virginia Woolf said that although a Hardy poem was on the face of it bad, it nevertheless achieved its own aim quite unmistakably.[5]

In the poems you've read, have you been able to see how this quirky language seems still to come out on top, presenting clear pictures and human feelings, or even – amazingly – by its strange sighing voice, a deep sense of song? Or perhaps you don't think it does and are wondering about Hardy by now. I suggest, however, that before going further with general speculation, we should now look briefly at a couple of poems to see how these effects work out. We need two, for so varied are Hardy's methods that few single ones would capture enough of his main techniques and devices.

Please now read, first, 'Life and Death at Sunrise' (p. 57). You may have already done so, because I mentioned it at the end of Chapter 3 (p. 37) if you remember, and have alluded to it since. However, I haven't assumed your knowledge of it yet, so now is the time to read it more closely. There is a useful wider discussion of it by Jean Brooks.[6] The only question I will put to you here, as with the next poem, is a general one. **How do you think the poem's language works? Look for both an overall general pattern and more detailed local examples. Use the list of categories given earlier in this chapter.**

DISCUSSION

The first two stanzas of this poem seem full of the abrupt stiff phrases we recorded above. The hills 'uncap' their tops at the start, and for a waggon to have a 'laboured leisurely jog' seems a contradiction. That the men 'halt of long use' (halt as they've so often done), and the birds 'try to entune at one time' (try to sing all together) could have been included in our list under point 8 or 9 above. Indeed, the couplet 'And look on the layers of mist/At

their foot that still persist' seems uncomfortably close in banality
to the World's Worst Couplet ('Across the vasty veldt/Their horses
they did pelt' – Alfred Austin, Poet Laureate from 1896). And
stanza one's last line 'Who gaze around to learn if things during
night have shifted' seems to precurse the Scottish clown-poet
William Macdonegall at the very Best-Worst he ever achieved.

Yet don't we at least get a vivid picture of the farmed and
hilly landscape on a misty dawn? But it turns out to be even more
than that. For at stanzas three and four we sense that something
far deeper may have been happening. We switch to the men
themselves talking, and we sense that much is already known. The
labourer's answer is, ' – 'Tis a boy this time. You've just met the
doctor trotting back./She's doing very well. And we think we shall
call him "Jack".' What is missing? Why, the word 'birth' of
course, as it is missing in the poem's title. And that the woman –
unnamed – already has a girl, and that the 'horseman' who came
'clapping down into the dip' was a doctor, which we weren't told
at first, just as we wouldn't know from our holiday caravan that a
passing local was the doctor, or anyone else.

In the fourth stanza the picture is rounded out at deeper level
still. It is now the waggoner's turn to ask, and the answer is 'Oh, a
coffin for old John Thinn:/We are just going to put him in.' We
see that the birth-death cycle is complete. A little chilling except
that the poem's close has, if not triumph, a certain assuredness;
but there is more yet. For, astonishingly, it dawns on us that the
hills' question at the start, whether 'things have shifted', was real.
They have and they haven't: a birth and a death: life's cycle has
gone on. And finally, don't we feel that this 'dawning' on us as
readers too has been the poem's entire drift and inference? The
dawning day had to dawn, in those oddly seen first pictures,
before in waking state the story could be told. It turns out almost
as though the poem began deliberately badly, so that the effect of
a growing clarity from dawn's light itself could come over us.
More widely then, Hardy's 'weird' language it turns out results
from his determination, at the start of the twentieth century,
to let language itself dawn; to leave its grammatical workings
uncovered, and as he himself frequently said, not burnish it over
with a fine veneer. You can try for yourself such analysis on the
more congested or oddly-expressed parts of Hardy's writing. 'On
the Esplanade', 'Overlooking the River Stour' and indeed 'God's
Funeral' (p. 230) are good examples. The last raises philosophical
topics which I raise in the final chapters.

Something intriguing arises from all this. Could it be that in
this poem 'Life and Death at Sunrise' Hardy is actually enacting a

principle that means a great deal to him personally? Might we say that the line 'woodlarks, finches, sparrows, try to entune at one time' is metaphor for just what Hardy is trying to do himself, with all his many tricks of writing and sources of language, all thrown together 'on one plane' as the contemporary writer William Archer put it of him?[7] Even more compellingly, can we tie this in with Hardy's sense of love, and failure in love? In 'A Countenance' (p. 352), which we discussed in Chapter 4, the poet was drawn to a laugh that 'was not in the middle of her face quite', and her too full lips. But the final word in that sentence feels not really in its right place quite, and it might seem that word and subject have become one thing rather more than we first thought. Again, the test of a consummate artist is that they also do what they say, they act it out in the words themselves, and you might like to consider this general idea at this point.

The context here is Hardy's many remarks about his preference for the imperfect, deliberately homely and unpolished, and we will return to that point shortly. First, however, we now need an example of the other main kind of writing we have touched on, and which reverses these trends. This is a more approachable kind of writing, common in love poems like 'A Countenance', and it was the tenor of the passage from 'Wessex Heights' cited above. It is littered all over the poetry, and is where people speak or feel simply, and no excessive irritating detail must be allowed to mingle with the purity of their mind and emotion.

Please now read the poem 'Near Lanivet, 1872' (p. 343). This, too, is what I would call a typical above-average Hardy poem; not maybe the greatest, but with much in it, usually all three ingredients of scene, dialogue and story. This particular poem depends more than usually on dialogue. **Again ask yourself the one question; how do you think the poem's language works? As with all Hardy poems bar very few (such as 'Paying Calls'), there is a certain accuracy in the phrasing which takes out any feeling of a full inspirational flow. But here it is not done by craggy or grainy vocabulary. How is it done? Again, consult the categories suggested earlier in this chapter.**

DISCUSSION

A man and woman are walking along a country lane, and the woman chooses to rest against a post with a crosspiece by the roadside. She realizes suddenly she must look like a crucifix, and this is unnerving. They walk on, brooding on this incident. I will suggest simply that the poem is about superstition, albeit that the characters are aware of it. The landscape itself is touched in in subdued fashion, kept out of the way. Words like 'crest', 'dusty way', 'solitude of the moor' are enough to tell us where we are. Accompanying them though is an equally backgrounded list of accruing words which quietly build to a feeling; 'weary', 'tired' 'sad' and so on. They make 'stunted' in the first line important in hindsight. But the pivot point comes at the end of stanza three and start of stanza four. 'And hurriedly "Don't", I cried' . . . 'I do not think she heard'.

What Millgate calls Hardy's marvellous poetic tact[8] takes us through this microscopic moment while leaving it in our minds as a direction to follow afterwards. By these few phrases, the man is paired with the woman. The line could have run, 'And sternly "Don't", I said.' But it doesn't. Instead, we feel he is anxious, for he answers 'hurriedly'; and he 'cries' rather than speaks. But the next half-line takes it further. For since the woman did not hear him speak, it follows that they both thought of the crucifix picture at the same moment, yet independently. This is another of Hardy's 'double visions' we mentioned in Chapter 3 (p. 36). Yet here the outcome is that the pair are tied in together, unable to escape the alarming implication that, if both thought of it at once, there may be something in the event to fear, whatever their rational objections. He tries to reassure her, but the bodily idea 'nailed' has already been uttered; and in a remarkable final touch, quite innocently, the poem ends simply 'Alas, alas', – twice, one for each of them. That they 'dragged on and on' then ties their walk to life's journey itself, and their weariness seems an allegory of all that is to come, or could come. Hardy's skill with the simple conjunctives and linking words of the language seems as practised as his use of the stronger nouns and adjectives of his already extensive vocabulary.

This kind of writing then is 'imperfect' too, in the different sense that it stands back from the richer words of the language's lexicon. I would like now to return to this point about imperfection, taking it however as only one of several principles the poetry embodies as far as its actual language is concerned. Again I hope you'll look for cases of this, or already have, including those where you think what I suggest doesn't meet the case, or goes too far.

1 First, this *imperfection* itself. Here are some of Hardy's own remarks: 'The whole secret of a living style and the difference between it and a dead style, lies in not having too much style – being, in fact, a little careless, or rather seeming to be, here and there. It brings wonderful life into the writing.' 'Inexact rhymes and rhythms now and then are far more pleasing than correct

ones.' 'The art (of poetry) lies in making (Nature's) defects the basis of a hitherto unperceived beauty.' 'Clouds, mists and mountains are unimportant beside the wear on a threshold, or the print of a hand'. 'To find beauty in ugliness is the province of the poet.'[9] In making such remarks Hardy descends directly from the principles of Gothic outlined by John Ruskin in the essay on Gothic touched on in Chapter 1. Ruskin wrote: 'Accept this then for a universal law, that neither architecture nor any other noble work of man can be good unless it be imperfect . . . if we pretend to have reached either perfection or satisfaction, we have degraded ourselves and our work'.[10] In this putting-away of satisfaction we see again the psychological thrust of Hardy's endlessly dissatisfied desires, as though there can be no disconnection between art and love.

2 A major result is the *loosely-slung* effect. In homely Hardyesque fashion, I think accurately too, it is what you could call the sack-of-potatoes effect. Donald Davie expresses doubt about this feature. 'Sometimes this is what offends us in Hardy's poetry . . . a shape *imposed* on the material, as it were with gritted teeth'[11] (his emphasis). One sees what Davie means, but I think he has reversed the process. Hardy doesn't impose his shape *on* the material; rather, he packs the material *into* the pre-chosen shape, as one throws clothes into a suitcase. The result is left loosely slung, not warped tight or wedged shut and immovable. The potatoes shake about in the bag, and one can feel their various shapes from outside. Hillis Miller made the same point. Usually, he says, the metre is 'an arbitrary framework into which certain material is pushed, trimmed to shape'.[12] That I think is more accurate than the imposition of a form. The resulting material, though 'trimmed to shape' certainly, retains its smaller individ-ualities within the larger pre-decided structure.

3 All of this yields the opportunity for *creative structuring* with which Hardy's poetry abounds. I will give the single example of rhyming. Again and again Hardy seems, at first reading, to put in a word or twist a sentence round just to get a rhyme that fits. It seems awkward. But the freedom from any feeling that it must sound 'natural' means that the poet has countless more words to choose from when looking for a rhyme. He is free to try any word to see if it yields up some new layer of meaning. In 'After the Last Breath' (p. 70) the first stanza ends 'no pillow sloped/Does she require'. It seems to be there just to rhyme with 'hoped'. But the vivid detail of what has gone on in the weeks before, endlessly having to punch up and freshen the sagging pillow the dying woman has rested on; this surely is a gain. In the poem just considered, 'Life and Death at Sunrise', the name 'John Thinn'

makes 'in' an easy rhyme, but it suggests too the skeleton inside the man who is dying.

These are just a few of the ways Hardy achieves his result; the lucid rendering of human and natural affairs and feelings in unique and disconcerting language. Imperfect, loosely slung and creatively structured are terms I have culled from others or made up myself. You can add or substitute your own. Either way, it is hardly surprising that the young Ezra Pound, who might seem to have had as different a poetic creed from Hardy's as could be imagined, could say on reading his poetry: 'Now *there* is a clarity. There is the harvest of having written 20 novels first'.[13]

7. The Wider Social and Cultural Background

It is now time to consider more generally how Hardy's poetry is related to the cultural movements and beliefs of his times.

'Near Lanivet, 1872' (p. 343), which we have just considered at the end of the previous chapter, is one of a few poems which feature the crucifixion. Two others are 'The Wood Fire' (p. 242) and 'In the Servants' Quarters' (p. 234). Each relates an incident before or soon after the crucifixion of Jesus Christ. The biblical story, and its reliability or otherwise, mattered very much to Hardy's contemporaries. What distinguishes these poems from their corresponding or similar passages in the Bible is their detailed realism. 'The Wood Fire', an invention, tells of a man whose job was to cut up the timbers of used crosses for firewood. He comments how some can be used again and how well they burn, and remarks that the crucifixions of 'last week-ending' were unusually troublesome. The crowd were jeering at the dying Galilean carpenter in the middle. 'In the Servants' Quarters' is not imaginary; it tells the story of Peter's denial of Jesus to save his own skin (see Matthew, XXVI, 69–75 and Mark, XIV, 66–72). But, although Hardy follows the story's sequence exactly (the three denials to the same three challenges) he still adds close microscopic detail. The girl 'flung disdainful glances', the constables laughed – and incidentally spoke in broad Dorset accent – and the girl noticed that Peter shuddered when he heard Jesus's chains clinking.

This insertion of exact detail into hitherto mythical or imaginary biblical stories cannot be understood without its nineteenth-century background. The Victorian age was the age of religious doubt; a gradual decline and ebb of belief in what had been regarded as divinely revealed certainties. Doubt focused most strongly on the story of the world's creation (in *Genesis*) and the divinity of Jesus Christ (in the New Testament gospels). The challenge to Genesis came centrally from Darwinism; the challenge to traditional views of Christ came from the new professionalism of historical scholarship.

The changing view of Christ concerns us here first. What theologians came to call 'the quest for the historical Jesus' had centred on the German university of Tubingen and one historian in particular, David Freidrich Strauss, whose *Der Leben Iesu (The Life of Christ*, 1836) was translated into English by the novelist George Eliot in 1845. The aim was to discover as much as conceivably possible of the actual historical life and death of Jesus Christ. But the very act of doing this meant that the image or aura of Christ might become secularized. The firmer the establishment of his undeniable existence, the more he might seem just an ordinary mortal, if a remarkable one. As a realist novelist Hardy had been much concerned with this matter of realism in religion. And so what matters in these poems is how he expresses a kind of respectful tribute to the gospel stories as themselves mythologically poetic, while distancing himself slightly from comment as to what was behind them. Hardy invents historical-type detail but keeps the story's main structure. Note that neither poem mentioned affirms, or denies, the nature of Christ.

As to the rise of positivistic natural science, Hardy himself claimed to be one of the very first readers of Charles Darwin's *The Origin of Species* when it appeared in 1859 when Hardy was only nineteen. Yet as Millgate points out it doesn't seem that Hardy was thrown into deep religious doubt by Darwin. It has also been pointed out recently[1] that even clergymen found belief in God and Jesus Christ compatible with both revised dating and evolution. One had only to put a moral connotation on evolution – that it enabled improvement for the better – to see it too as part of God's purpose in creating the world. Indeed at the end of *In Memoriam* Tennyson had resolved the poem's religious doubts by seeing creation as evolving toward a perfect and divinely intended goal. The doubts about the historical figure of Christ were more damaging, and Hardy seems to touch on them in such poems as 'The Oxen' (p. 229) and 'The Impercipient' (p. 228). In 'God's Funeral' (p. 230) the poet says, of the dead god, 'I did not forget/That what was mourned for, I, too, long had prized.' Again you might like to consider this, for Hardy tells us too that, while a clergyman friend had said 'The Wood Fire' described 'probably what happened', one critic had described it as 'revolting'.[2] There is little doubt of the impact the new historical studies made on the aura of Christ's divinity.

More generally though you might wonder about the tone of 'The Oxen', 'The Impercipient' and similar poems. They seem less hostile than regretful. Many Victorians felt such regret. James Mill and his son John Stuart Mill felt that the practice of religion in the world had been an unmitigated evil, but they did not stretch these views to include the life of Jesus Christ himself, nor indeed God, if God existed. Hardy seems to have had mixed experience of the clergy. For example there was the bishop W. Walsham How, who burned *Jude* in public, but there were Hardy's clerical friends the Moule family too who would have done no such thing. But in general, the expression was muted. Hardy's poem 'God's Funeral' was attacked as atheistic by G. K. Chesterton, but Hardy himself denied the charge, as he did numerous similar charges. Like many other Victorian intellectuals Hardy maintained a dual attitude.

The difficulty, which survives today, was as follows. To many people the new materialist natural sciences in general implied a wholly physical explanation of human existence. Yet human beings, apparently unlike the animal realm, possessed both self-consciousness and a sense of value; of better and worse, both morally and aesthetically. One might insist that every single feature of human activity, including love and knowledge, could be finally described in terms of the movements of atoms, particles, and (later) genetic structures. But that still didn't seem to explain how we could deeply *feel* that an action was good, or bad, just or unjust and the like. If all was merely a swirl of plant-like growth how could something be ethically 'better' than something else? How could killing a fellow human be 'bad' if we couldn't say a bird eating a worm was also bad, and if ultimately we were descended (via apes) from birds and worms?

On the matter of consciousness, the case commonly cited –

which I think clearly influenced Hardy – was that of the eyeball. The 'argument from design' maintained that so intricate and astonishing an object must have been created by an intelligent god. The argument from evolution held that thousands of tiny modifications and refinements, over millions of years, could have brought elementary nervous systems to a point where they could see the shapes and colours made apparent by light. But that still did not explain how human beings could *know* they were 'seeing' something, any more than a telescope or camera could. These difficulties were resolved, at least for some, by postulating a 'double layer' of evolution in human beings. Our evolution was both physical and social-ethical. The development of consciousness had meant a gradual awakening in *homo sapiens* to known social existence, and a need in it for altruism and moral values above those of the animal or plant world. It was then only a step to saying that 'religion' was merely a mythological structure demanding obedience to the higher ethical principles which distinguish humans from animals, and personifying those principles as powerful superhuman entities – gods. Such views led to that prominent group of Victorian philosophers and social commentators known – then, and to Hardy, as now – as social meliorists. They held that human societies could be based on wholly secular values hitherto thought of as religious in origin. We referred to the meliorists briefly in Chapter 2 (p. 19): the French sociologist Auguste Comte, Herbert Spencer, John Stuart Mill, and also perhaps Thomas Henry Huxley, friend and champion of Charles Darwin, whom later Hardy himself became friendly with.

As a young man Hardy read and later always adhered to much in their writings. He repeatedly refers to their views in his prose writings and letters. Hardy hoped the church could be retained but as a centre for broad social and moral teaching rather than exact religious doctrines and dogmas. Comte called such a position the 'religion of humanity'; Comte founded a church of that name and a similar attitude was held for a long time by the novelist George Eliot among many others. In a letter to Edward Clodd who had published a biography of T. H. Huxley in 1902 Hardy wrote,

> What is forced upon one again, after reading such a life as Huxley's, is the sad fact of the extent to which Theological lumber is still allowed to discredit religion, in spite of such devoted attempts as his to shake it off. If the doctrines of the supernatural were quietly abandoned to-morrow by the Church, & 'reverence & love for an ethical ideal' alone retained, not one in ten thousand would object to the readjustment, while the enormous bulk of thinkers excluded by

the old teaching would be brought into the fold, & our venerable old churches and cathedrals would become the centres of emotional life that they once were.[3]

No doubt Hardy was nostalgically trying to keep the church he loved while recognizing his doubts about its teaching. (Note here again the numerous poems Hardy wrote set in churches; for example 'The Impercipient', 'In Church', p. 121, 'A Church Romance', p. 60, 'The Chapel-Organist', p. 142, 'The Abbey-Mason', p. 130, 'The Country Wedding', p. 187, and many others.) But the theme remains; keep the churches, but emphasize morality not dogma. It is the continued attempt to take account of the dual-level evolution of *homo sapiens* referred to above. In his preface to *Late Lyrics and Earlier* Hardy stated this general double ethical objective of human endeavour. It is that 'pain to all upon [this globe], tongued or dumb, shall be kept down to a minimum by loving-kindness, operating through scientific knowledge, and actuated by the modicum of free will conjecturally possessed by organic life when the mighty necessitating forces – unconscious or other – that have "the balancings of the clouds", happen to be in equilibrium.'[4]

Referring to this same passage later, in 1922, he writes to a friend Lady Grove that 'I thought my meaning to be clear enough that some form of Established ritual & discipline should be maintained in the interests of morality, without entering into the very large question of what that form should be'.[5] Back in 1885 he had confided to the publisher John Morley, 'I have sometimes had a dream that the church, instead of being disendowed, could be made to modulate by degrees (say as the present encumbents die out) into an undogmatic, non-theological establishment for the promotion of that virtuous living on which all honest men are agreed – leaving to voluntary bodies the organization of whatever societies they may think best for teaching their various forms of doctrinal religion.[6]

And yet this dual picture runs into its own contradictions. A 'meliorist' wants things better and believes this can be achieved by social policy. Yet Hardy was incessantly accused of pessimism. Having read as much as you now have, which side would you go for? Much of the Preface to *Late Lyrics and Earlier* is an answer to these very charges of pessimism, and you would I think derive much interest from reading it. (It is printed in full at the end of our selection; on pp. 442–50.) It does seem undeniable, despite Hardy's protestations, that many of the poems we have looked at imply that one is better off out of this world ('Wessex Heights',

p. 293; 'Friends Beyond', p. 182), or that we don't understand our
situations, or that fate almost inevitably takes the saddest turn
against us. A key poem here is 'The Mother Mourns' (p. 243),
which expresses some qualms about the dual-level of evolved
human existence.

The 'mother' in the poem is nature, although she comes in as
a disembodied voice, merely 'A low lamentation . . . Perplexed,
or in pain'. The Mother's lament is that the human race was
originally created as simply a part of nature, but has now out-
grown that, and itself envisages futures outside what nature
originally intended. The 'range of his vision/Now tops my intent';
furthermore, humans think that given the basic materials their
now developed brains could 'evolve a creation/More seemly, more
sane' than the one nature herself produced. Humans indeed now
actually despise nature:

> He holds as inept his own soul-shell –
>   My deftest achievement –
> Contemns me for fitful inventions
>   Ill-timed and inane

The Mother ends up regretting ever having made such a creature,
and plans in future to stick to 'mildews and mandrakes,/And slimy
distortions . . .', i.e. the base orders of the primal insect and reptile
kingdom.

The question is of how this account can be read without
inherent contradiction. For one cannot see in it the meliorists'
ordinary dual-level view of evolution, that of physical and social-
moral evolution occurring in convenient tandem, with the former
as a kind of support base for the latter. If Darwin and the evolutionists were right, 'Nature' originated the human race; yet here
is Nature herself bewailing her action in doing so. She does
so furthermore because humans are doing the very things the
meliorists recommend; a creation 'More seemly, more sane'. Is the
suggestion then that in so aiming humans are going against
the very origins the Darwinists have discovered they come from?

Hardy went into these matters deeply. Again his letters and
other writings attest to this. The pessimistic philosophers, notably
Schopenhauer but also Nietzsche, were among the authors he
thoroughly absorbed. In 1924 he writes to a friend of a book
about his own (Hardy's) work which, said one reviewer, was 'a
little too much like a treatise on Schopenhauer with notes on
Hardy'. Hardy complains that 'as my pages show harmony of
view with Darwin, Huxley, Spencer, Comte, Hume, Mill, and
others (all of whom, as a matter of fact, I used to read more than

Sch.) my kinship with them should have been mentioned as well as with him'.[7] And, in now looking back over the poetry we have read with these views in mind, we can discern a number of ways in which these questions became poetically embodied.

Let's consider those capital-letter entities again. They particularly appeared if you remember in 'Nature's Questioning' (p. 288). In that poem, creatures and objects in nature wistfully wonder if an Automaton or some Vast Imbecility or perhaps some Plan is the universe's guiding principle. In the poem 'To My Father's Violin' (p. 67) there is something similar. The dead father resides in the (capitalized) Nether Glooms and Mournful Meads. These capitals seem to attribute entity, reality, to such categories while not elaborating them theologically; in fact they seem to have it both ways. I suspect Hardy's longing for churchyard skeletons to speak to him was similar. He yearned not merely for an afterlife, but also that reality itself should be eternal and in some way god-directed. (The tendency may be associated with the Victorian trend for seances, attempts to communicate with the recent dead through a human medium.) However, the chief of these capitalized personifications is the Immanent Will. This curious entity, along with attendant beings (Chorus of the Pities, Spirit of the Years, and so on) Hardy placed at the centre of his long poem *The Dynasts*, and he worked out its details with considerable philosophical accuracy. The Immanent Will seems to be a compromise between a personal god and the physical life-force in which an atheist believes who also, however, holds that the universe is a single energized unit.

The Immanent Will combines two main characteristics; a blind force, yet with some embryonic consciousness of itself. In the latter respect it is extremely close to the 'Absolute Thought thinking itself' conception of the major early nineteenth-century German philosopher G. W. F. Hegel (1770–1831). Hegel – anticipating and influencing Karl Marx – believed history was a single, unilinear sequence of unrepeatable events. The universal power behind history and the universe was, in effect, one colossal 'thought' gradually, through the passing aeons of the universal time-span, becoming aware of its own existence; and the moment of that awareness's dawning was now. Hardy's view is most remarkable. 'That the Unconscious Will of the Universe is growing aware of itself I believe I may claim as my own idea solely'.[8] Since Hardy wrote that to a friend in 1907, which was over seventy years after Hegel's death, it is surprising that Hardy (and incidentally some of his commentators) should claim it for himself, especially since Hardy had read some of Hegel in earlier

years. Nevertheless, there in black-and-white the idea stands, and
has obvious relation to a general philosophy of evolution.

We can now tie these ideas in with Hardy's poetry, and this
brings us back to the eyeball. The 'Immanent Will' that Hardy
postulates, is blind. He doesn't say so in so many words, but the
point is clear enough. Since the Will is only *becoming* conscious of
itself (even in 1907!) it cannot be thought able to see, i.e. have
conscious awareness of, anything else either. Again one thinks of
the camera and the telescope. Such devices 'see' objects in one
sense, but do not know that they do. And we are at once back,
of course, in our discussion about seeing and unseeing, which
occurred in Chapter 3. You may remember that I asked you
whether there wasn't a sort of knowing 'blindness' in Hardy's
poetry (p. 31). You will also remember how often the question
came up, of the difference in Hardy's poems between 'seeing'
literally with the eyes (as in 'On the Departure Platform', p. 364)
and seeing with the mind or feelings, as when we say, I see, I get
the point, I see what you must be going through. In 'Nature's
Questioning' the natural objects and creatures wondered if they
were the remnants of a god dying top-down, 'brain and eye now
gone'. This may seem 'pessimistic'; the Immanent Will becoming
conscious of itself might seem happier. Either way the point
remains; if we can't feel, and don't have consciousness, then
seeing with our eyeballs is meaningless.

But this is not just a quibble over the word 'seeing'. It is vital
for the evolutionist. If the eye evolved over a thousand stages,
from the most elementary nerve-cells to when you can *see* your
beloved disappear down the departure platform, when did consciousness enter the process? Was there one single point, or a
period? Did the increasing power of sight lead to the mind's new
sensitivity, or the reverse? The debate over eyesight continues
today, with a well-known account by Richard Dawkins in his
book *The Blind Watchmaker*.[9] Dawkins argues that the eyeball
developed through evolutionary stages without benefit of a divine
intelligence or some comparable source.

Such questions had already been raised, about eyesight, in
Darwin's *The Origin of Species*. In the sixth chapter there is a sub
section called 'Organs of extreme perfection'.[10] That title shows
how important evolutionists thought it was to explain something
as delicate and subtle as the eye. You may be thinking by now that
I am overdoing attention to this matter of the eyeball itself. It is a
metaphor, after all, of awareness, of consciousness. But the whole
point is that it is *not* just a metaphor. The question is, how can the
eye see, if there is no consciousness behind it. Can you see when

you are asleep? Or dead, but with your eyes open? Can a camera tell you what it is seeing, or what it feels like to see it? These debates about eye and eyesight are at the heart of the evolutionists' debate about how far the benevolent mind of God entered the making of organs like the eye itself. And it lurks not far behind every one of all those occasions when Hardy evoked 'seeing', literal or otherwise, in his poems on understanding and apprehension. (Tom Paulin's book on Hardy's poetry contains a chapter called 'Perception' where these matters are discussed.[11] You might like to consult it.) And this observation brings me to the last but, perhaps, most significant observation this chapter will attempt to introduce.

The late nineteenth and early twentieth century were remarkable not only for debating theology and evolution. They also witnessed many new technologies and sources of energy, from the large-scale like the railway down to the everyday such as the telephone and the improvement of the already-existing camera. Technology is present in a number of poems. For example there is 'The Photograph' (p. 326), 'Faintheart in a Railway Train' (p. 317) and indeed 'On the Esplanade' (p. 323), where the lights on the boulevard are strung up right round the bay. There are numerous others and you may have found some, such as 'Midnight on the Great Western' (p. 158) and, very differently, the war poem 'And there was a Great Calm' (p. 285). There is the channel ferry in 'The Contretemps' (p. 148), the nineteenth century ironworks there and in 'The Harbour Bridge' (p. 175) and the modern guns in 'Channel Firing' (p. 278). A certain feature of this kind of technology and its poetic presentation is now highly relevant. If you haven't already done so, please now read the poems 'The Convergence of the Twain' (p. 277) and 'And there was a Great Calm'. What strikes you about them, especially in light of their length?

Surely the point is that, contrasting their length, they seem to hover round or come upon a single instant. In the first poem the two main objects, the great ocean liner the *Titanic* and the huge iceberg, meet at a single second. It is marked in the poem by 'Now!' at the end, a second of zero-time which 'jars two hemispheres'. In the second poem the whole of the First World War, and the years of peace following it, are divided by the single point of time at which the armistice came into effect and 'all firing stopped'. How effectively Hardy underlines that instant of silence by a case of the armistice being broken: 'One checkless regiment slung a clinching shot/And turned'; one final blast before the end. These two poems repay close reading for their imagery, their vivid sense of things meeting, colliding and parting, and a deep philosophy underlying all. But the crucial point relates to the capture, by this means, of the entire nature of modern technology. The matter has been considered by the German Marxist critic Walter Benjamin.[12] Benjamin does not refer to Hardy, but he wrote in the early 1930s, a little after Hardy's death.

Benjamin distinguishes between the *shock* and the *aura*. A 'shock' is a significant event of instant time, as opposed to, for example, events found at the basis of natural or seasonal change. An 'aura' is the pervasive atmosphere that surrounds something slower in its emergence. It hangs round a masterpiece of painting or architecture, or a known landscape. But the (small) shock is occasioned by much modern-world technology: the instant snapshot, the striking of a match, the switching off of a car engine, the turning on of a light, the ringing of a telephone or the postal telegram (cf. the poem 'A Wife in London' – p. 257 – and consider the order in which the two pieces of news are announced), the start-up of a huge factory machine-plant. One might add from our time the demolition of a piece of woodland by bulldozers, or the impact of headline news on a TV bulletin. These 'shocks' are central to the modern sensibility.

Benjamin illustrated his point by showing that the first photographs attempted to emulate paintings. We mentioned Hardy's deep interest in painting in his London period in Chapter 2 (p. 15). The classic pose of the subject in early photography, in mournful or hazy atmosphere, was typical. This was rudely counteracted by the French photographer Atget, who in about the year 1900 began to take shots of deserted street scenes (the word 'shot' well suits our theme here). These scenes did not compare with paintings, which were done to be hung in private houses and attract a sense of remembrance or awe. Rather they were for exhibition in galleries; they were meant for mass reproduction, and felt less like art than like evidence. You may already have thought of how poems like 'The Contretemps' (p. 148) or 'Faintheart in a Railway Train' are closer to such scenes than to paintings.

Are not the many 'incidents' that Hardy's poems record, such shocks and camera-shots, or at least have that feeling? Is not 'A Thunderstorm in Town' (p. 358) such a thing; and indeed wasn't the sequence of poems resulting from the shock of Emma's death an enlarged version of a comparable event? Isn't that why it didn't come over as a traditional and slower elegy? The point relates to all we have been saying, not only about eyesight and the eyeball. If all we can see – however clearly – is a series of disconnected fragments, then we are not 'seeing' life in any wider sense at all.

Camera accuracy, as we said in Chapter 3, only increases the wish for full understanding; it doesn't itself give that understanding. And this seems to show how Hardy's poetry is a response to the theory of evolution and the decline of traditional religion too. For if there ceases to be a central, overriding moral authority from above, which pervades our lives, then the poet's residual task – so thought Thomas Hardy – is to record 'unadjusted impressions',[13] those many fleeting moments, just as they are, 'forced on us by chance and change'. Our lives in this modern age cannot it seems be slow unfoldings of the seasons, of natural country or even town life based upon a few humanly developed but fundamentally rooted institutions such as government, money, home life, community, education and religion. The pace and direction of change are too sharp. The poet can only seize and record the instants as they go by. Hardy called his resulting poems his 'unadjusted impressions', and enhanced this effect by his deliberate lack of veneer (his word) and verbal polish. The poems are comparable to the straightforward camera-click rather than the elaborate and skilled work of the oil painter, building the painting over quite long periods of time. Of course the photographer is skilled; so is Hardy's kind of poet.

Benjamin takes the matter further in a different essay on Baudelaire which is also relevant here. Benjamin developed Sigmund Freud's views on the nature of memory. Freud argued that only unconsciously, never consciously, could a perception be registered by the mind and stored for a long time to become, not a memory, but a remembrance. As we saw earlier, Hardy would resurrect such memories years after their occurrence and make them into poems. But the function of consciousness, Freud argued, is not to absorb stimuli but protectively to resist them. In a world of 'shocks' – numerous incessant small stimuli – the consciousness must work all the harder; it becomes what Benjamin here calls 'presence of mind' and is the mode by which – up to the arrival of video – we have watched films.

But if the consciousness of these shocks resists them rather than internalizing them, they do not build up to an overall deep sense of the world. And this, it might seem, is what Hardy's poetry results in; his endless fleeting glimpses don't of themselves build up a total picture or philosophy. The events themselves, as we have suggested, are 'not seen'; the eyeball stares at them blindly. It is only when the grey gloaming comes, the melancholy mood and the failure to notice all, as in 'On the Esplanade' or 'Overlooking the River Stour' (p. 346) that a deeper self-awareness is achieved. Rather, the impression itself is captured and made to last, just as the photograph, once taken, can be kept in the album forever. Yet its subject, the car passing the traffic-light or the athlete crossing the line, remains always the fleeting glimpse it was at the moment when it was taken. For this reason, as Hillis Miller suggested, few of Hardy's poems make us stay with them. It is not because they poetically fail, but the reverse; we want to run on to the next, to see whether it can find a solution the previous one did not.

At the heart of the enterprise of Hardy's poetry then, I suggest, is a positive spirit. It is the philosophical unknowing we discussed and saw in the chapter on love. The endless quest to light on something that would resolve our difficulties; this is what the poetry seeks, apparently never to find. Its human appeal perhaps lies in that we know it won't be found, but that the search is genuine and human, and one we make ourselves in ordinary life. Curiously, this may lead to the final suggestion that Hardy is not, after all, a pessimist. You may by now have formed your own views on this matter. I would again adduce a part of Freud's theories, this time on the death wish.[14] For Freud the death wish is occasioned because the conscious organism longs to return to a stable state, to reach a point where the endless stresses and tensions have gone away. But by always continuing his search for the ideal loved woman or adequate philosophy beyond, Hardy and anyone like him are resisting this option.

For the achievement of Victorian positivistic science was to find a way of seeing the world as though it actually were in the state the death wish longs for; dead-as-a-withered-leaf, material, metallic, unsinging. This has been a great gain in material clear-sightedness away from superstition. In practical usefulness the gain, as the meliorists and Hardy wanted, was that such a science would relieve the distress of suffering people. But along with that material discovery there relentlessly survived this yearning for an alternative to the gods who had lost credibility; a moral order, or a social and ethical aspiration. In Hardy's poetry we see it in the capitalized entities which survive the gods' disappearance; we see it in the ghosts, the dim but comforting churches, the reliable even if cold and unknown landscapes. And we see it too in his endless recording of the daily small incidents, tiny 'shocks', in which the newly changing actions and sufferings of thousands of people coped with the incessant tide of change.

8. Critical Responses

In the foregoing chapters I have tried to suggest something of what I make of Thomas Hardy's poetry, and perhaps what you might too. But what have others made of it?

There is one particularly strange response to Hardy's poetry. In his introduction to our selection David Wright wrote: 'All this [preceding comment] makes Hardy sound as if he were a difficult poet to read; the paradox is, he is not. It is only difficult to make up one's mind how good, and/or how bad, almost any particular poem of Hardy's is' (p. 16). The same surprising admission was made more than thirty years ago by the American critic Mark Van Doren: 'I have heard it [said that] too many of Hardy's poems are not 'good'. And I agree; but I am always changing my mind as to which ones those are . . .' Van Doren goes on to conclude that 'the building as a whole should be left just as it lies'; that is to say, selections of the 'best' of the *Collected Poems* cannot be attempted successfully.[1]

This is appealing but surely curious. That a poet should be thought to vary in standard is common enough. That readers should disagree as to which poems are good and bad is also understandable. But for experienced readers and critics to feel quite powerfully that they themselves don't know whether such poems are good or bad – that surely suggests either total uniqueness in the poetry or perhaps a certain wiliness in the author! Some critics, both his supporters and his detractors, have faced this squarely and stated that Hardy quite simply is like that. The work may seem awkward, quirky, stumbling, but it turns out to last in our minds despite that quality. We already mentioned T. S. Eliot and Virginia Woolf as examples of this (p. 70), but I also like the response of the writer Katherine Anne Porter: 'What could be duller? What could be more labored . . . ? Except for this in my memory: . . . I have seen it, I was there'.[2] It seems the poet must have recognized his limitations and used some other ingredient,

some special angle, to achieve something memorable after all.
That critics found it hard to say what this was, led to the very
slow start toward building a body of insightful criticism on the
poetry. As Davie put it in 1972, confronted by Hardy's poetry
'one honest critic after another has by his own confession retired,
baffled and defeated'.[3] As Tom Paulin has put it, 'The poems are
so various that no one has found a consistent way of approaching
them'.[4]

   Possibly Hardy's rather selective use of his own chief poetic
influences – Wordsworth, Shelley and Browning – was distracting
to the earliest critics. Dennis Taylor believes that Wordsworth
is the chief presence behind Hardy's writing. Wordsworth saw
nature as the great beneficent source of worthwhile human
feelings. He therefore wrote his poetry in 'the language of men' as
he called it,[6] instead of any artificial 'poetic diction', which tends
to occur when a civilization believes itself to be moving on from
nature. Despite broad sympathy with this, and the sense still of
nature as our home, Hardy began to feel nature was inadequate
as a source of perfection and beauty. The ' "simply natural" is
interesting no longer' . . . 'Nature's defects must be looked in the
face and transcribed' . . . 'I think the art lies in making these
defects the basis of a hitherto unperceived beauty'.[7] Such a view
could hardly appeal to critics identified with either the romantic
school of nature or the aesthetic school of civilization – both
predominant at the end of the nineteenth century.

   The Shelley influence on Hardy has been strongly championed
by Harold Bloom, who has himself produced a unique theory
of poetic influence generally.[8] Many critics attempt to trace
influences, but Bloom argued that the poet feels the need to shrug
off such influence as dangerous to his own claim to originality.
Bloom notes that Hardy may seem scarcely like Shelley on the
surface, but 'poetic influence has almost nothing to do with the
verbal resemblances between one poet and another' (p. 19).
According to Bloom Hardy was overwhelmed by Shelley in the
1860s. But Hardy reacted against the power he felt in Shelley
while still continuing to write about the things (birds, wind,
nature's forces) ecstatically evoked by Shelley in his odes. Hardy
did so, however, merely to record his own different feeling of
deadness, or of a broken-backed vision of such things. Again, later
critics saw this as a negative response.

   Browning's dramatic monologues were useful models to
Hardy in more direct fashion. Browning's many long verse stories
are usually told in the voice of a single narrator, who however
also seems to have someone close by in the room or street listening

to it all. This approach was one possible modification of the single, individual voice, the ego's 'I', of the romantic poets.[9] We have seen Hardy's propensity for narrative in many poems, and there is also the frequent claim to being 'dramatic' which Hardy makes in his Prefaces. But the immense zestful energy of Browning's vocabulary is again missing from Hardy. Hardy's narratives often turn on a single fateful event, leading to tragedy or more mundane collapse; a seemingly pessimistic sense that things will turn out wrong but quite ingloriously too. This too seemed to earlier critics a betrayal of poetry's vocation, which, they felt, should suggest a robust human stoicism or even heroism in the face of natural calamity.

So when we come to how the first critics assessed Hardy generally, we find considerable bafflement. We cited a few cases of this in Chapter 1 (p. 8). In 1902 an anonymous critic in *The Athenaeum* wrote (of Hardy's *Poems of the Past and the Present*) that Hardy 'is almost wholly devoid of the faculty of self-criticism. The diction is persistently clumsy, full of ugly neologisms, with neither the simplicity of untutored song nor that of consummate art'. An interesting exception to this hostile response to Hardy was the poet Ezra Pound. Pound saw, quite simply, that Hardy doesn't fit into any category easily; rather, what he does is done with the greatest clarity. This quality naturally appealed to the poet who more than any other had asked for precision and exactness in poetry, as against the Victorian fustian which he detested and through his programme of Imagism sought to eradicate. However, in 1915 it seems that Lytton Strachey also understood what Hardy was trying to do.

> [Hardy's lapses] are not merely superficial and occasional blemishes; they are in reality an essential ingredient in the very essence of his work . . . He is incorrect, but then how unreal and artificial a thing is correctness! . . . All the taste, all the scholarship, all the art of the Poet Laureate seem only to end in something irremediably cold and remote; while the flat, undistinguished poetry of Mr Hardy has found out the secret of touching our marrow-bones.[10]

Yet very few critics saw it this way. In the 1930s, for example, the American poet R. P. Blackmur was still sceptical. So when Philip Larkin wrote his essay 'Wanted: Good Hardy Critic'[11] in the 1960s, his title only reflected what many people felt; namely, that this vast body of work had been enjoyed and examined only to the point where certain main issues were raised but not resolved.

Then, in 1961, came the first thorough study of the poetry as a whole, by Samuel Hynes.[12] This book can still be strongly recommended, for Hynes was among the first to evaluate the poetry sympathetically on its own terms, rather than solely as a late appendage to the work of a major novelist. Hynes demarcates both Hardy's use of philosophy and his supposedly inadequate language. In these two areas he grapples with the bewilderment that greeted Hardy as a poet for many years.

Hynes's argument about Hardy's philosophy is, roughly, that because of the perplexing language many readers had read the poetry for its philosophical import alone. Hardy, however, could never build a philosophical attitude in a single poem, because his sensibility was always drawn towards irreconcilables. Thus, in the Hegelian terms Hardy knew and Hynes uses, Hardy would put thesis and antithesis into a poem but with no synthesis, no resolution. (This duality is comparable to the 'double vision' idea of Hillis Miller, as we shall see.) Yet this very failure, and its unpretentiousness, Hynes argued produced a great sadness and beauty, supported by the almost perverse consistency [*sic*] of Hardy's body of work. This consistency refers less to merit than to absence of development. The whole career feels broadly the same. Some critics recently have argued against this, notably Dennis Taylor; but the difficulty is that so many of Hardy's poems are simply undateable. If there were clear development and change from one period to another dating would surely be possible. Hardy had a thirty-year poetry career with probably another thirty years before it containing occasional poetic bursts.

As to Hardy's style, Hynes suggested its strength could be seen on different lines from those normally associated with poetic writing. Hardy's style is a knowing accident; it comes from truth, and belief in what one is writing. The wide range of Hardy's vocabulary, and the odd way he treated it as all the same, itself creates its own magnetizing effect.

In practice therefore Hynes opened up two possible lines of more positive critical assessment of Hardy, according to these two features of Hardy's philosophy and his language. Philosophically, one has to see that Hardy presents dramatically the impossibility of coherence in the modern world, if one is true to one's impressions (Hardy's own frequent term). As to language, one must see that Hardy's 'awkwardness' is itself his aesthetic aim; he almost leans over backwards to prove that the unpolished object is the more humanly approachable. As a result, criticism of Hardy's poetry has been able to develop.

So much is groundwork. But then in 1973 came Donald Davie's *Thomas Hardy and British Poetry*.[13] Davie's book begins with a statement of far-reaching implications with an altogether new emphasis. The book intends to 'illustrate a thesis: that in British poetry of the last fifty years (as not in American) the most far-reaching influence, for good or ill, has been not Yeats, still less Eliot or Pound, not Lawrence, but *Hardy*' (p. 3).

The emphasis is Davie's. The warning note 'for good or ill' turns out to mean, not that Davie simply sees Hardy as a bad influence and nothing more, but that a certain lowering of sights is what characterizes the Hardy mode, and that this perhaps is what lies behind the debate about Hardy's badness, carelessness, and everything else. Only the Introduction and the first two chapters deal with Hardy himself. The remaining chapters explicate the extent to which later poets, most notably Larkin, have been influenced by Hardy. Davie's tone is robust and his mode of writing vigorous and highly readable. It is disconcerting if refreshing to hear that 'at prosody Hardy beats Yeats hands down' (as in poker or darts perhaps) and that the view of an earlier critic must be 'scotched'. But beyond doubt Davie put Hardy on the agenda as a poetic force no longer to be ignored.

Davie's argument centres on the incursion of Victorian technology in Hardy's lifetime. Davie couples this with the view of Hardy we expressed in the previous chapter, that he was strongly influenced by the meliorists of the Victorian age. However, Davie uses the phrase 'scientific humanism' to describe Hardy's social views, and sees this in political terms as liberal. In short, it is new technology, properly applied, that will bring social improvements.

These new technologies were mentioned in the last chapter – the photograph, harbour bridge, war machine, railway train, electric light and the rest. Davie, quite reasonably, centres on large-scale engineering itself. Hardy is 'the poet of technology, the laureate of engineering . . . (his poetry's) effective aesthetic is that of industrial technology in the age of heavy engineering.' But Davie then argues, not that Hardy is responding psychologically or philosophically to technology, but that Hardy's poems are themselves pieces of technology. Citing 'The Wind's Prophecy' (p. 331), 'The Convergence of the Twain' (p. 277) and 'Lines to a Movement in Mozart's E-Flat Symphony' (p. 344), Davie finds in their imagery and shape a use of metallic material and an engineered structure. The *Titanic* poem 'itself is an engine, a sleek and powerful machine; its rhymes slide home like pistons inside cylinders, ground exactly to fractions of a millimeter'.[14] In the poem on Mozart 'what one hears is not the chip-chip of a mason's chisel, but a clank of iron girders swung down from a crane; not Gothic architecture at all but specifically Victorian architecture, the iron bridges and railway stations of engineers like Brunel and

Smeaton'. And in 'The Wind's Prophecy' Davie sees the 'glint', the 'muddy monochrome' and the 'smitings' and 'hammerings' as all emerging from the heavy-metal materials of the same technological activity.

Davie's deduction from his view about Victorian engineering is then tied to his own response to the poetry's overall feeling. Hardy is a 'technician' and indeed 'honest journeyman'. His poems are made to do a workmanlike job, they round off their main central point in each case in good mechanic's fashion and pass on to the next. Their stance is humble, and again and again the poet 'bows and retires (when another poet would) advance and take us by the throat' (p. 36). This then is the secret of Hardy's 'carelessness' or awkwardness; and while it has, as Davie acknowledges, both immense skill and fundamental honesty, it represents 'a crucial selling short of the poetic vocation, for himself and his successors' (p. 40).

Davie's intent is positive; his next chapter entitled 'Hardy Self-Excelling' looks at the poems he sees as more successful because more ambitious and fully-worked ('After a Journey', p. 381; 'Wessex Heights', p. 293; and 'During Wind and Rain', p. 419); and finally he suggests that Hardy's liberalism could itself be what limited him. This liberalism furthermore strongly contrasts the markedly illiberal stances of the other main early twentieth-century poets Davie cites – Pound, Eliot and Yeats. Such poets were of course sceptical of scientific humanism. They believed rather in a combination – varying from poet to poet – of the achievements of traditional and classical civilization and religion. I confess to being rather sceptical of Donald Davie's view, but I hope you will go to these poems and see how this absorbing theory strikes you. But I also feel a counter-view is needed, which will at least give you the opportunity of making a straight comparison.

Here we enter a contemporary school of literary criticism, that of deconstruction. Deconstructionism is a complex matter and I have to sketch in briefly here a few of its chief characteristics.[15] Deconstructionism focuses on writing itself, the very act (physical and mental) of inscription on the blank page, on the blankness before inscription occurred. It sees writing as an act inherent in itself; it is in part playful; and it is not merely the transcription to paper of thoughts, feelings or images in the mind beforehand. Writing is its own action: it goes on forward – or rather sideways – from phrase to phrase. It is an endless deferring of final meaning, rather as Hardy's loves and poems both are also an endless deferral of completion to the next glimpsed woman or the next poem itself. For such reasons the deconstructionist sees no clear boundary between poetry and other writing, or indeed any writing type and any other, another point of interest when we consider Hardy's dual literary career and its components. The kind of mechanical finished accomplishment Davie suggests is at complete odds with this view of writing. Far from 'bowing and retiring' being the reason for Hardy's apparently unconcerned or shrugging attitude, it is that no poem can ever be complete, as a human rendering, in its very nature. This takes us back to a number of considerations.

There is first of all Davie's view of Hardy as poetic engineer. This is clearly at odds, as Davie says, with the view of Hardy as Gothic. But it also contests a view put forward by the structural anthropologist Claude Lévi-Strauss,[16] himself precursor to deconstructionism, though it must be said Lévi-Strauss is regarded as now outmoded by them for that very reason. But an influential distinction Lévi-Strauss made at a central point in his work was between that of the scientist (or engineer) and the *bricoleur*. The scientist/engineer takes raw material and makes it into an object or machine from a clear, abstract design. So are Victorian bridges, railways, electric lights and so on also made. The *bricoleur*, by contrast, takes objects *already* in a certain condition and uses them, as they already are, to make what is wanted in hand-to-mouth fashion. Let's take a homely example like a hen-house. The scientist/engineer gets a 'pure' hen-house design, and buys the raw materials to make it; wood in exact lengths, glue, plastic roof sheeting and so on. The *bricoleur* gets what he already has – maybe a rusty bedstead, a couple of bits of glass from disused picture-frames, and an old car's tyres to stand it on. In more theoretical terms: the scientist takes a structure and makes an event: the *bricoleur* takes an event (thing already made, bedstead, picture-frame) and makes from it a structure. The scientist's 'event' is its newness.

Which process do you think most describes Hardy's poetry? *Bricoleur* or scientist? Davie says the scientist, but one could surely as well argue that Hardy's craggy awkwardness, derived from his finding of old words, hymn tune forms, stories for the narratives and so on, go to making those poems that feel more like travel bags full of joggers and first-aid kits. Can we really say that many of his poems are sleek engineering jobs humble or not? I leave this decision to you.

Another mode of approach to this, again along deconstruction lines, would be through what in an earlier chapter, following Hillis Miller, we called the 'double vision'. We can now see that this view is similar to that of Samuel Hynes, cited above, when he suggested that the poems always offer Hegel's standard thesis and antithesis, but with no synthesis. Many of Hardy's poems seem to see a matter first from one point of view, then from another. Very often the two are balanced symmetrically. We cited 'The Sunshade' (p. 138) as a clear example, and larger-scale ones are 'Near Lanivet, 1872' (p. 343), where the two characters independently recognized the crucifixion stance, and of course 'The Convergence of the Twain', where the two fated items of iceberg and ship, one mobile, one static, come to their destiny from existentially balanced positions.

But this 'double-vision' element can be seen, in somewhat metaphysical terms you may think, as containing the very mark, trace or rupture on the face of blankness that deconstructionists argue is the nature and condition of writing. The phrase 'mark, trace, rupture' derives from the work of the French deconstructionist philosopher Jacques Derrida, whose writings have themselves been so controversial in British and American literary criticism in the last two decades.[17] Writing is a fundamental act of conscious existence. There is blankness, of paper, life, air or anything else, and then there is event, signification, sign or mark on it. Derrida also uses the word 'hinge' for this elemental mark. An event of historical significance, for example, is a 'hinge' or turning-point across the blank face of otherwise 'empty' historical time. My argument then is that these poems of Hardy's, and surely virtually all but a very few have this characteristic, are themselves a series of 'marks', small incidents, events, aspects quickly seen and point taken, across the face of a kind of sea of sad, otherwise meaningless reality. Each poem is 'marked' by a kind of line down the middle, separating the two parts of the double vision. But equally and more generally, to 'write' them is, simply, to write; Hardy sets his poems down, in whatever form comes to hand, and moves on. This kind of poetry is thus like 'writing' is for Derrida in general. One writes a phrase, and writes the next one sideways on to it, the next one sideways to that, and so on. There may or may not be some underlying 'shape' to writing; that is left with the reader to decide or impose. This view seems to square with the further view of J. Hillis Miller in his book[18] on Hardy where again the continuous deferral from poem to poem, and the relatively undifferentiated significance from poem to poem across the whole body of work, is what counts. The view surely takes us back to that of David Wright and Mark Van Doren, cited at the start of this chapter. It is difficult to say whether any poems are 'better' than any other, for all seem to have this departure-from-themselves, this leaving the scene sadly only at the moment when, too late, the implication dawns.

And that last remark, about an implication dawning 'too late', seems central to the views expressed by Denis Taylor (1981). We mentioned it at the end of Chapter 5 (p. 63) and must elaborate it further now. Taylor characterises Hardy's typical lyric as an incident that recapitulates a life. That is to say, an incident, usually an 'interruption' to something else more stable or reliable, forces the poet to look back over time and see anew – but 'too late' – the significance of something past. But the distance in the past may be a few minutes, or years or decades. In 'Overlooking the River Stour' (p. 346) the poet gave a detailed description of the beautiful river scene before him, only then to realize what he had ignored in human terms in the house behind. The deconstructionist would certainly note the double meaning of 'over-looking' here, declaring furthermore that we do not need to believe that the poet (who is always the blind seer) himself knew what he was saying. It is a further tenet of deconstruction that writers unknowingly but necessarily subvert their own text as they write. The absence of an overall shape means that a variety of interpretations is always possible for any piece of writing.

But Taylor's point goes wider. Indeed it complicates the picture a little, although I would suggest fruitfully. For Taylor I think does feel that the *Poems 1912–13* are the centre of the whole work. They are the big, central rupture or interruption in Hardy's life which set him toward full understanding, for the rest of his poetic life, of what its significance had been for himself as husband, writer, career man, novelist. I have twice now used the word 'interruption'; it is Taylor's word, and useful it surely is. There is often an interruption within the poem. The lovers' walk is suddenly interrupted by their seeing that one of them looks like a crucifix. The poet reading at a lamp is interrupted by the arrival of insects through the window on to his page. But *Poems 1912–13* records, starkly and suddenly, the 'interruption' of a lifetime, the death of a near companion whom one has perhaps ignored. This approach to the matter is perhaps one way of resolving the dilemma of whether these poems are the central group in Hardy's work. One may think they are the finest achievements poetically in any event; but even if one does not, they may be seen as central in a different sense, the 'hinge' round which the whole body hangs and swings.

And this brings us back to Hegel. As said in the previous chapter (p. 81) Hegel believed that time is continuous and on-going, with the universal consciousness becoming aware of itself

but not yet having done so fully. In earthly terms ,'on the ground'
so to speak, this worked itself out for Hegel in the feature that, as
Hegel put it, 'the owl of Minerva flies out at dusk'. That is to say,
an era or generation cannot know itself until it is over. The owl is
the bird of knowing; Minerva was the goddess of wisdom. Understanding is achieved, but 'too late'; but it is achieved. Hardy,
perhaps from pessimism, perhaps from a sense of the right shape
of his characteristic poem, left the understanding for the reader, or
sketched it in briefly at a poem's close, or by implication.

I suggest then only that Davie's belief about the importance
of pragmatic technology in Hardy's poetry, needs to expand to
account also for its central act of seeing, and its tone as human
feeling. Davie's view of Hardy as social democrat, reasonable as
far as it goes, simply misses out the entire dimension of feeling and
vulnerability for which Hardy is read; the sadness, the godless
landscape, the lost opportunity, the missed love.

The term 'double vision', the inability to reach synthesis, is
clearly related to the deeper matters of vulnerability in deferred
desire and missed love. It might therefore finally be considered in
light of one of the most prominent branches of literary criticism of
the last two decades: feminism. By its nature it is surely pertinent
to Hardy, but by its own historical occurrence feminism is also of
the post-modern period. Feminism takes out the more question-
able virilities of earlier ages, including those to which Hardy
objected. But, as we saw in the chapter on love, Hardy's search
was for the feminine aspect of things; it was a search he never
expected to consummate. There are intriguing references to his
attitude in his relations and correspondence with the Victorian
man of letters Sir Leslie Stephen. Hardy reported Stephen as
saying that, like Hardy himself, he read novels by women to learn
about 'the things that go on at the back of women's minds'.[19]

Hardy, by contrast but not contradictorily, said that women
taught him what books couldn't. Elsewhere and later he suggested
that women and knowledge had an ambivalent relation. Some
knowledge is shielded from women (though doubtless the Victorian
milieu was responsible for what truth lay in that), while other
knowledge is known to women alone. In 1893 Hardy wrote a
short story which included a wedding. He wrote to Florence
Henniker asking for help with the bride's thoughts of the wedding
morning: 'Please insert in pencil any details that I have omitted, &
that would only be known to a woman.' Many years later, Hardy
complimented Florence Henniker on a short story she had written
herself. He noted in it especially 'the modern, intelligent, mentally
emancipated young woman of cities, for whom the married life

you kindly provide for her would ultimately prove no great charm – by far the most interesting type of femininity the world provides for man's eyes at the present day.[20] It has been frequently said that this obliquely refers back to the intriguing Sue Bridehead of *Jude the Obscure*. Sue Bridehead was of course the last fictional woman Hardy produced before switching to poetry full-time. It is arguable that this elaboration of this character was, in some way, a predisposing factor in that switch. Hardy once called himself 'a young man at fifty'; he was a little older than that when the switch to poetry came. Hardy's 'interest in women', to use that totally inadequate phrase, seems inseparable from his turning to the lyric form, his withdrawal to Dorchester, perhaps his marital unhappiness, and, I suggest finally, his great interest to us now, in a post-modernist phase of our own culture, in which women are playing an increasingly public part.

Hardy's approach to women, discussed in Chapter 4, seemed always to end in the deferral of satisfaction of desire. Love never arrives, or if it does it fails. A number of poems seem to contain a symbol for this. They are the ones which refer to an unborn, illegitimate or stillborn child. 'A Trampwoman's Tragedy' (p. 115), contained this feature. So do 'A Hurried Meeting' (p. 176), 'Julie-Jane' (p. 92), 'A Wife and Another' (p. 160) and various others. Thomas Hardy and Emma Gifford had no children. Despite certain rumours, it is doubtful if Hardy sired any by anyone else. And children generally – i.e. not babies but young children playing, or the older sons and daughters of married couples – scarcely figure in the poetry at all. From a feminist viewpoint Susan Friedman has interestingly investigated the metaphor of childbirth as prototype for a largely male creative art. Artists have been described, by male critics, as having pregnancy, labour, giving birth, and the rest.[21] Friedman cites T. S. Eliot as saying that, when a poem is finished and published, he felt like telling it to 'go away' if it reappeared before him on paper or in consciousness. One similarly tells an annoying child, however much loved, to 'go away'. But Hardy throws his poems away in the act of writing. He doesn't 'educate' them or resolve them into maturity. Nor did he labour; he once said that he never redrafted a poem more than twice, for fear of losing its freshness. As already suggested, they are endless, low-key vocabularied deferrals of the resolution the poet needs for his constant unfulfilled desires. The lack of fulfilment is also, however, a deferral of desire's death. It may be that we await now a fully feminist critique of Hardy's poetry, which would show how his poetry both moves toward the female and yet stays short of it; writes his maleness, but in full recognition of its incomplete nature as expression of a full humanity. That was perhaps the essence of Thomas Hardy's double vision.

I hope this relatively brief thesis on Hardy's poetry has been valuable to you in your explorations of his continually rewarding body of work. I hope too that you will benefit, as I have, from the rapidly increasing body of writing about that work, which I have referred to in these pages.

Notes and References

Chapter 1: First Selection

1 F. E. Hardy *The Life of Thomas Hardy 1840–1928* (Macmillan, 1962), p. 105.
2 F. R. Leavis *New Bearings in English Poetry* (Peregrine Books, 1963; first published by Chatto and Windus, 1932), p. 54.
3 To be accurate, Maugham said this not about Hardy but about Edward Driffield, Maugham's own fictional character portrayed in Maugham's novel *Cakes and Ale*. Driffield is commonly said to be modelled on Hardy (though Maugham denied it) and the description I reproduce here has stuck.

Chapter 2: Main Events in the Life

1 Reprinted in the *Thomas Hardy Society Journal*, vol. VII, no. 1, pp. 10–15.
2 *Life*, p. 386.
3 Robert Gittings, *Young Thomas Hardy* (Penguin Books, 1978) and *The Older Hardy* (Penguin Books, 1978); Michael Millgate *Thomas Hardy* (Oxford University Press, 1982).
4 Millgate, pp. 114–15.
5 In *The Genius of John Ruskin: Selections from His Writings*, ed. John D. Rosenberg (Routledge and Kegan Paul, 1979), pp. 170–95. (*The Stones of Venice* was first published in 1853.)
6 Millgate, p. 516.
7 These and other remarks of Hardy's on poetry and art are usefully assembled in *Thomas Hardy: Poems*, ed. James Gibson and Trevor Johnson (Macmillan Casebook Series, 1979), Part I. Many are also to be found in the text of Hardy's poetry edited by T. R. M. Creighton (see Bibliography), Appendix II.
8 Millgate, p. 57.
9 Millgate, p. 297.
10 Gittings, *Young Thomas Hardy*, pp. 313–23.
11 Ibid., pp. 90–93.
12 William Morgan 'A Calendar of Hardy's Dated Poems' (unpublished). I am most grateful to Professor Morgan for kindly lending me this list.

13 Millgate, p. 321.
14 *Thomas Hardy: Selected Letters*, ed. Michael Millgate (Oxford: Clarendon Press, 1990), p. 51; Evelyn Hardy *Thomas Hardy: A Critical Biography* (Hogarth, 1954), p. 260.
15 *The Older Hardy*, p. 121.
16 *Letters*, p. 261.
17 In fact it seems to recur in stanza three of 'The Going' (p. 370) and perhaps in 'The Spell of the Rose' (p. 387). Many of Hardy's note-book entries and passages from letters could be the material for his poems. The point is germane to his methods of working, for example this passage:

> A good story or play might run as follows: A certain nobleman, a widower, has one son, a young son now lying at (25) the point of death. The nobleman his father is an old man, in great trouble that there will be no heir in the direct succession. Son dies. Among his papers are found a girl's letter – the letter of a girl whom the son had begged his father to keep from want, as he had seduced her. The father finds that she is going to have a child. He marries her, parting from her at the church door. He obtains an heir of his own blood.

From *The Personal Notebooks Of Thomas Hardy*, ed. Richard H. Taylor (Macmillan, 1978), p. 14.
18 *Letters*, p. 263.

Chapter 3: Seeing

1 For example the famous description of Tess walking in Blackmoor valley, chapter XVI in *Tess of the D'Urbervilles*. To a watcher from the hills above she looked like a fly on a billiard table. Also the remarkable opening scene in *Far from the Madding Crowd*, where Gabriel Oak peers at two women through a hole in a building's wall. The next day he conceals himself to watch a girl (Bathsheba Everdene) riding a horse, but stretched out flat on her back, imagining herself unseen.
2 Rosemary Sumner, 'Indeterminacy in Hardy's Novels and Poetry', *Thomas Hardy Society Journal*, vol. V, no. 2, pp. 33–45.
3 John Henry Newman, *Grammar of Assent* (Image Books, New York, 1955), ch. vii, s. 2, p. 206.
4 J. Hillis Miller, *Thomas Hardy: Distance and Desire* (Harvard University Press, 1970), chs 2 and 3.
5 Jeremy Hooker, *The Poetry Of Place* (Manchester: Carcanet Press, 1982), p. 13.

Chapter 4: Love

1 Millgate, pp. 510, 565; cf. also Gittings, *the Older Hardy*, p. 184.
2 See note 12, ch. 2 above.
3 Tom Paulin *Thomas Hardy: the Poetry of Perception* (2nd edn, with new Introduction, Macmillan, 1986), p. 90.

4 Ibid., p. 132.
5 Miller, *Thomas Hardy: Distance and Desire*.
6 cf. Jacques Lacan, *The Four Fundamental Concepts of Psychoanalysis*, trans. Alan Sheridan (Penguin Books, 1979) esp. ch. 15; also *Ecrits: a Selection*, trans. Alan Sheridan (Tavistock, 1977) esp. ch. 9. cf. also Elizabeth Wright, *Psychoanalytic Criticism: Theory in Practice* (Methuen, 1984) esp. ch. 7.

Chapter 5: Death

1 Millgate, p. 378; *Life*, pp. 209–10.
2 Robert Circasa, 'Thomas Hardy's Poems of 1912–13: the Engagement of Loss' in *Concerning Poetry*, vol. V, no. 19, pp. 95–106.
3 J. Hillis Miller, 'Topography and Tropography in Thomas Hardy's "In Front of the Landscape"' in *Post-structuralist Readings Of English Poetry*, ed. R. Machin and C. Norris (Cambridge University Press, 1987), pp. 332–48.
4 Dennis Taylor, *Hardy's Poetry 1860–1928* (Macmillan, 1989), p. 107. For the ghost incident itself see Millgate, p. 528.
5 See note 12, ch. 2 above.
6 Paulin, op. cit., pp. 205–12; Taylor, op. cit., pp. 30–38; Donald Davie *Thomas Hardy and British Poetry* (Routledge and Kegan Paul, 1973), pp. 59–60; Harold Bloom *A Map of Misreading* (Oxford University Press, 1975), pp. 17–24.
7 Millgate, p. 516.
8 Miller in Machin and Norris, p. 341; Taylor, p. 24.
9 Miller in Machin and Norris, esp. pp. 341–44.

Chapter 6: Language

1 Dennis Taylor, 'The hunting of the *OED*' in *Annals of Scholarship*, vol. VII, no. 2, 1990, p. 158.
2 From *The Faber Book of Ballads*, ed. Matthew Hodgart (Faber and Faber, 1965), p. 180.
3 Paulin, p. 3.
4 Samuel Hynes, *The Pattern of Hardy's Poetry* (University of North Carolina Press, 1956), ch. 6.
5 In J. Gibson and T. Johnson, pp. 62–6. For the Eliot and Woolf quotations see Ralph W. V. Elliott, *Thomas Hardy's English* (Basil Blackwell, 1984), p. 15.
6 Jean Brooks, 'The Homeliest of Heart-Stirrings: Shorter Lyrics' in Gibson and Johnson, pp. 202–16.
7 Archer's famous comment on Hardy's language first appeared in the *Daily Chronicle* on 21 December 1898.
8 F. E. Hardy, *Life*, p. 335.
9 Gibson and Johnson, pp. 29, 30; 'Notes from Hardy's Journals' in *Thomas Hardy*, ed. Samuel Hynes, Oxford Authors Series (Oxford University Press, 1984), pp. 485–90.
10 Ruskin, p. 184.
11 Davie, p. 16.

12 Miller in Machin and Norris, p. 333.
13 *The Letters of Ezra Pound*, ed. D. D. Paige (New York, 1950), p. 294.

Chapter 7: Wider Social and Cultural Background

 1 Grevel Lindop, 'Newton, Raymond Tallis and the Three Cultures' in *Poetry Nation Review*, vol. 18, No. 1, Sept–Oct 1991, p. 40.
 2 *Letters*, p. 371.
 3 Ibid., p. 145.
 4 Our text: *Thomas Hardy: Poems*, ed. David Wright (Penguin Books, 1978), p. 445.
 5 *Letters*, p. 371.
 6 Ibid., p. 40.
 7 Ibid., p. 386.
 8 Millgate, p. 450.
 9 Richard Dawkins, *The Blind Watchmaker* (Longman, 1986).
10 Charles Darwin *The Origin of Species* (first published 1859; Penguin Books, 1968), pp. 217–24.
11 Paulin, ch. 1.
12 Walter Benjamin 'The Work of Art in the Age of Mechanical Reproduction' and 'On Some Motifs in Baudelaire' in *Illuminations*, trans. Harry Zohn (Collins/Fontana Books, 1973), pp. 219–54 and 157–202.
13 From Hardy's Preface to 'Poems of the Past and Present', in *Thomas Hardy: Selected Poems*, ed. David Wright (Penguin, 1978 – present text); p. 442.
14 Sigmund Freud, *Beyond the Pleasure Principle*, The Pelican Freud Library, ed. Angela Richards, vol. XI (Penguin, 1977).

Chapter 8: Critical Responses

 1 In Taylor, *Hardy's Poetry 1860–1928*, p. xxiii.
 2 In Ralph W. V. Elliott, *Thomas Hardy's English* (Basil Blackwell, 1984), p. 16.
 3 Davie, p. 13.
 4 Paulin, p. ix.
 5 Dennis Taylor, 'Hardy and Wordsworth' in *Victorian Poetry*, 24 (1986), pp. 441–54.
 6 William Wordsworth, 'Preface to Lyrical Ballads' in *The Prose Works of William Wordsworth*, ed. W. J. B. Owen and Jane Worthington Smyser (Oxford: Clarendon Press, 1974), pp. 118–65.
 7 *Life*, pp. 185, 114.
 8 cf. note 6 ch. 5 above.
 9 I have discussed this briefly in John Powell Ward *The English Line* (Macmillan, 1991), pp. 64, 79. cf. also Carol T. Christ *Victorian and Modern Poetics* (University of Chicago Press, 1986) esp. ch. 2.
10 In J. Gibson and T. Johnson, pp. 52 and 64.
11 Philip Larkin 'Wanted: Good Hardy Critic' in *Required Writing: Miscellaneous Pieces 1955–1982* (Faber & Faber, 1983), pp. 168–

174. R. P. Blackmur, 'The Shorter Poems of Thomas Hardy' in *Language as Gesture* (Harcourt, Brace and Co., 1952).

12　Samuel Hynes, *The Pattern of Hardy's Poetry* (University of North Carolina Press, 1961).

13　Donald Davie, *Thomas Hardy and British Poetry* (Routledge and Kegan Paul, 1973) esp. Introduction and Ch. 1, 'Hardy as Technician'.

14　Ibid. p. 17.

15　For a general introduction cf. Christopher Norris, *Deconstruction* (Methuen New Accents, 1982).

16　Claude Lévi-Strauss *The Savage Mind* (Weidenfeld and Nicolson, 1966), pp. 16–36.

17　Jacques Derrida, *Of Grammatology*, trans. G. C. Spivak (Johns Hopkins University Press, 1974) esp. ch. 2; *Writing And Difference*, trans. Alan Bass (Routledge and Kegan Paul, 1978) esp. ch. 9.

18　See note 4, ch. 3.

19　*Letters*, p. 237.

20　*Letters* pp. 90 and 240.

21　Susan Stanford Friedman, 'Creativity and the Childbirth Metaphor: Gender Difference in Literary Discourse' in *Speaking of Gender*, ed. Elaine Showalter (Routledge, 1989), pp. 73–100.

Bibliography

Texts

1 Main text used (see Note at the beginning of the book):

Thomas Hardy: Selected Poems, edited with an Introduction by David Wright, *The Penguin Poetry Library* (Harmondsworth: Penguin, 1978).

2 Complete editions of Thomas Hardy's poems:

Thomas Hardy: The Complete Poems, edited by James Gibson, (London: Macmillan New Wessex Edition hardback, 1976; London: Macmillan Papermac Edition, 1981). Both editions are notably inexpensive. They include all the poetry apart from *The Dynasts*.

Thomas Hardy: The Complete Poetical Works, edited in 3 volumes by Samuel Hynes (Oxford: The Clarendon Press, 1985). These are excellent editions, but are rather more expensive, being available in hardback only.

A particular advantage of the collected editions is that they arrange the poems in the order in which they were originally published, and in the various individual volumes.

3 Other selections of Hardy's poetry:

Thomas Hardy, edited with an Introduction by Samuel Hynes: Oxford Authors Series (Oxford: Oxford University Press, 1984).

This edition contains about five hundred of the poems, arranged according to Hardy's original individual collections. They include Hardy's original Prefaces to those collections, and a selection of other prefaces and literary comments by Hardy.

Poems of Thomas Hardy: A New Selection, selected with an Introduction and Notes by T. R. M. Creighton (London: Macmillan, 1974).

This selection has about three hundred poems, arranged by the editor under various headings: love, nature, dramatic, and so on. It also contains an unusually large selection of quotations from Hardy's writings about poetry and art, and all the prefaces, and a useful introduction by the editor.

4 Standard recent edition of Hardy's epic is:

Thomas Hardy, *The Dynasts, with an Introduction by Harold Orel* (London: Macmillan, 1978).

Biography and Letters

Thomas Hardy: Selected Letters, ed. Michael Millgate (Oxford: Clarendon Press, 1990).
The Personal Notebooks of Thomas Hardy, ed. Richard H. Taylor (Macmillan, 1978).
F. E. Hardy, *The Life of Thomas Hardy 1840–1928* (Macmillan, 1962). (This book was effectively written by Thomas Hardy himself.)
Robert Gittings, *Young Thomas Hardy* (Penguin Books, 1978).
Robert Gittings, *The Older Hardy* (Penguin Books, 1978).
Michael Millgate, *Thomas Hardy* (Oxford University Press, 1982).
Evelyn Hardy, *Thomas Hardy: a Critical Biography* (Hogarth, 1954).
Robert Gittings and Jo Manton, *The Second Mrs Hardy* (Heinemann Educational, 1979).
Thomas Hardy's England (Jonathan Cape, 1984), written and compiled by John Fowles and Jo Draper.

Critical Studies of Hardy's Poetry

Books exclusively or substantially on Hardy's poetry
Ralph W. V. Elliott, *Thomas Hardy's English* (Basil Blackwell, 1984). Outstandingly useful guide to Hardy's vocabulary and language use. Deals with poetry and novels alike.
Thomas Hardy: Poems: A Selection of Critical Essays, ed. James Gibson and Trevor Johnson (Macmillan, Casebook Series, 1979). Useful compendium of Hardy's own critical comments, early criticism of the poetry, and later responses.
Samuel Hynes, *The Pattern of Hardy's Poetry* (University of North Carolina Press, 1961). The first major and still highly useful guide to Hardy's poetry.
Tom Paulin, *Thomas Hardy: the Poetry of Perception* (2nd edn, with new Introduction, Macmillan, 1986), p. 107. Unusual and winding but approachable and stimulating study.
J. Hillis Miller, *Thomas Hardy: Distance and Desire* (Harvard University Press, 1970). Major treatment of novels and poetry alike from leading American contemporary theoretical critic.
Dennis Taylor, *Hardy's Poetry 1860–1928* (2nd edn, Macmillan, 1989). Beyond doubt the outstanding recent treatment of Hardy's poetry. Stimulating and thorough.
Dennis Taylor, *Hardy's Metres and Victorian Prosody* (Oxford University Press, 1988). Valuable authoritative study on this aspect of the subject.

Books containing main sections Hardy
Donald Davie, *Thomas Hardy and British Poetry* (Routledge & Kegan Paul, 1973) esp. chs 1 & 2. Stimulating and renowned thesis on Hardy's poetry.

F. R. Leavis, *New Bearings in English Poetry* (first published by Chatto &
Windus in 1932; Peregrine Books, 1963) esp. ch. 2.
John Powell Ward, *The English Line: Poetry of the Unpoetic from
Wordsworth to Larkin* (Macmillan, 1991) esp. ch. 7, 'Thomas
Hardy'.

Journals devoted to Hardy

The Thomas Hardy Society Journal edited until 1990 by James Gibson:
from 1990 by Norman Page. Wide-ranging journal on biographical
and critical aspects.
Agenda, vol. X, nos 2–3, Spring–Summer, 1972 (special issue on
Thomas Hardy). Articles by Thom Gunn, C. H. Sisson, David
Wright, Charles Tomlinson, Donald Davie and others.

Articles on Hardy's poetry

R. P. Blackmur, 'The Shorter Poems of Thomas Hardy' in *Language as
Gesture* (Harcourt, Brace & Co, 1952).
Jean Brooks, 'The Homeliest of Heart-Stirrings: Shorter Lyrics' in Gibson
and Johnson, pp. 202–16.
Robert Circasa, 'Thomas Hardy's Poems of 1912–13: the engagement of
loss' in *Concerning Poetry*, vol. V, no. 19, pp. 95–106.
Henry Gifford, 'Hardy in His Later Poems' in *New Pelican Guide to
English Literature*, ed. Boris Ford (Pelican Books, 1983, vol. VII,
From James to Eliot), pp. 166–79.
Brian Green, 'Darkness visible: defiance, derision and despair in Hardy's
"In Tenebris" poems' in *Thomas Hardy Society Journal*, vol. VI,
no. 2, 1990, pp. 126–46.
David Holbrook, 'Thomas Hardy and the meaning of existence' in *Lost
Bearings in English Poetry* (Vision Press, 1977).
Irving Howe, 'The Short Poems of Thomas Hardy' in *The Southern
Review*, Autumn 1966, pp. 878–905.
Philip Larkin, 'Wanted: Good Hardy Critic' in *Required Writing: Mis-
cellaneous Pieces 1955–1982* (Faber & Faber, 1983), pp. 168–74.
J. Hillis Miller, 'Topography and Tropography in Thomas Hardy's "In
Front Of The Landscape"' in *Post-structuralist Readings of English
Poetry*, ed. R. Machin and C. Norris (Cambridge University Press,
1987), pp. 332–48.
William Morgan, 'The Partial Vision – Hardy's Idea of Dramatic Poetry'
in Gibson and Johnson, pp. 244–52.
John Peck, 'Pound and Hardy' in *Agenda*, vol. X, nos, 2–3, Spring–
Summer 1972, pp. 3–10.
Rosemary Sumner, 'Indeterminacy in Hardy's Novels and Poetry',
Thomas Hardy Society Journal, vol. V, no. 2, pp. 33–45.
Dennis Taylor, 'Hardy and Wordsworth', in *Victorian Poetry* 24 (1986),
pp. 441–54.

General Literary Theory

Harold Bloom, *A Map of Misreading* (Oxford University Press, 1975).
Jacques Derrida, *Of Grammatology*, trans. G. C. Spivak (Johns Hopkins
University Press, 1974) esp. ch. 2.

Jacques Derrida, *Writing and Difference*, trans. Alan Bass (Routledge & Kegan Paul, 1978) esp. ch. 9.

Jacques Lacan, *The Four Fundamental Concepts of Psychoanalysis*, trans. Alan Sheridan (Penguin Books, 1979).

Jacques Lacan, *Ecrits: a Selection*, trans. Alan Sheridan (Tavistock, 1977).

Claude Lévi-Strauss, *The Savage Mind* (Weidenfeld & Nicolson, 1966).

Jean-Francois Lyotard, *The Postmodern Condition: a Report on Knowledge*, trans. Geoff Bonnington and Brian Massumi (Manchester University Press, 1984).

Jan Montefiore, *Femininism and Poetry* (Pandora Books, 1987).

Christopher Norris, *Deconstruction* (Methuen New Accents, 1982).

Elizabeth Wright, *Psychoanalytic Criticism: Theory in Practice* (Methuen, 1984).

Wider References

The Faber Book of Ballads, ed. Matthew Hodgart (Faber & Faber, 1965).

Walter Benjamin, 'The Work of Art in the Age of Mechanical Reproduction' and 'On Some Motifs in Baudelaire' in *Illuminations*, trans. Harry Zohn (Collins/Fontana Books 1973), pp. 219–54 and 157–202.

Carol T. Christ, *Victorian and Modern Poetics* (University of Chicago Press, 1986) esp. ch. 2.

Richard Dawkins, *The Blind Watchmaker* (Longman, 1986).

Charles Darwin, *The Origin of Species* (first published 1859; Penguin Books, 1968).

Susan Stanford Friedman, 'Creativity and the Childbirth Metaphor: Gender Difference in Literary Discourse' in *Speaking of Gender*, ed. Elaine Showalter (Routledge, 1989), pp. 73–100.

Sigmund Freud, *Beyond the Pleasure Principle*, The Pelican Freud Library, ed. Angela Richards, vol. XI (Penguin, 1977).

Jeremy Hooker, *The Poetry of Place* (Manchester: Carcanet Press, 1982).

Grevel Lindop, 'Newton, Raymond Tallis and the Three Cultures' in *Poetry Nation Review*, vol. 18, no. 1, Sept–Oct, 1991.

John Henry Newman, *Grammar of Assent* (Image Books, New York, 1955).

John Henry Newman, 'On the development of Christian Doctrine', written and published in 1845.

Ezra Pound, *Selected Prose 1909–1965*, ed. William Cookson (Faber & Faber, 1963).

The Letters of Ezra Pound, ed. D. D. Paige (New York, 1950).

The Genius of John Ruskin: Selections from his writings, ed. John D. Rosenberg (Routledge & Kegan Paul, 1979).

Dennis Taylor, 'The hunting of the *OED*' in *Annals of Scholarship*, vol. VII, no. 2, 1990.

William Wordsworth, 'Preface to Lyrical Ballads' in *The Prose Works of William Wordsworth*, ed. W. J. B. Owen & Jane Worthington Smyser (Oxford: Clarendon Press, 1974), pp. 118–65.

Index